MORE
BILL BRAMAH'S
ONTARIO

BILL BRAMAH

CANNONBOOKS

TORONTO

ABOUT THE AUTHOR

For more than 15 years, Bill Bramah has appeared as Global TV's roving reporter, bringing human interest items to viewers in Canada, the United States, and Australia. His wife Jenny is the show's tireless Production Assistant, contributing to the research and writing. Together, they have travelled hundreds of thousands of miles throughout Ontario, discovering interesting and unusual people and places.

The selections in this volume were chosen from the stories that Bramah has written during the last three years. His other books include *Bill Bramah's Ontario* and *Bill Bramah's Nooks & Crannies*.

DEDICATION

To Jenny, who has been with me since the beginning.

CANNONBOOKS
25 Connell Court. Unit 2
Toronto, Ontario M8Z 1E8

© 1991 by Bill Bramah

Canadian Cataloguing in Publication Data
Bramah, Bill, 1915-
        More Bill Bramah's Ontario

1st ed.
ISBN 0-9695251-0-9

1. Ontario - Biography - Anecdotes. 2. Ontario-
History, Local - Anecdotes. I Title.

FC3061.8 B73 1991 971.3'002 C91-093921-7
F1057.6.B73 1991

Printed and Bound in Canada by Metropole Litho Inc.
Design and Production by Michael Waldin

First Printing: April, 1991

Front Cover Photo: Bill Bramah in front of a 19th Century log cabin at the
Markham District Historical Museum, Markham, Ontario
Back Cover Photo: Bill Bramah and his wife Jenny stand in a refurbished
General Store at the Markham District Historical Museum.

Cover photos by Mark Zelinski.
Special thanks to Birgitta MacLeod, Education Programme Coordinator at
the Museum, for her assistance with the photography.

TABLE OF CONTENTS

❂ ❂ ❂

❂ ❂ ❂

❦ ❦ ❦

❦ ❦ ❦

Introduction

❦

There must be a lot of the gypsy in my soul. Even as a child, I was one of the roving kind. I became well known at the Lost Children's Centre at the C.N.E. where I was always assured of getting an ice cream cone while waiting for my long-suffering mother to pick me up. And I was a regular at the Playland on the roof of Eaton's downtown store where lost children were taken in the old days. It wasn't that my mother was careless. It was just that I was a very elusive little kid, and an incurable dreamer who would wander willy-nilly.

When I grew up I changed jobs frequently although staying mostly in the same media field. But 15 years ago, I finally found my niche as a roving reporter for Global News. It was right down my alley.

Since then, with my wife Jenny, who's a production assistant, I've roamed the province doing T.V. items about interesting and unusual people and places. We have travelled hundreds of thousands of miles in our Global wagon visiting towns and villages throughout the length and breadth of Ontario. Eventually, the stories were turned into a segment on the news called "Bramah's Ontario".

We stay in hotels and motels in various areas and have our favourite stopovers where the innkeepers have come to know us well. We have a farm on Southern Georgian Bay near Penetanguishene but don't get there very much. Jenny says, "it's where we keep our furniture".

We get leads for stories from letters people send us, or weekly newspapers, or telephone calls, or often just from someone we meet on the street or in a restaurant. We seldom go to the city. It takes us about two days to research a story and get it in script form. When we're ready to shoot, veteran cameraman Terry Culbert, who's been with us for the past ten years, comes from Toronto, shoots the story and takes it back to Global for editing. We hit the road again. Along the way, I rewrite the stories for a syndicated newspaper column and for books.

This is the third book about our travels, about the people we've met and the places we've visited. We hope you enjoy reading about them. Who knows? There may be a lot of the gypsy in you, too.

Bill Bramah

The Old Cider Press

❧

I've put the bite on plenty of apples in my day. Filched them from Niagara Peninsula orchards as a youngster, in later years bought them by the bushel at city fruit markets, and now occasionally wander in our own small orchard on an autumn morn and gently pick off a rosy, juicy-looking apple to savour its goodness and sense the bounty of the harvest.

The trees have been there for well over 70 years. Their gnarled, crooked branches reach out as in a Disney fantasy. The old trees are proud survivors of the merciless northwest winds that sweep down into Southern Georgian Bay and across our farm near Lafontaine.

The apples are of the Wealthy variety and make delicious apple pie, but this year Jenny thought we might have some pressed into cider.

We were heading for Eastern Ontario, one of the province's big apple growing areas, so we picked a bushel from the old trees, and put it in the back of the van, hoping we'd find a cider press in our travels.

Along the way, we stopped at the village of Tyrone, north of Bowmanville, to do a story about an 1846 waterpowered mill we'd heard about. Robert Shafer, the young heritage-conscious owner, gave us a brief tour of the ancient structure and explained it was one of the few remaining mills of its kind in the country.

Robert was busy, as was his small staff. But not milling flour or cutting logs. They were lugging apples to a cider press set up in another part of the building!

It was an unexpected coincidence. Jenny went out to get out apples while I took a closer look at the cider press.

It was ancient, big and bulky. The apples were being washed as they rumbled up on a conveyor to a grinder and we could see the mash dripping down. Layers of it were wrapped in nylon cloth. The layers were separated by wooden racks and put under 14 tons of pressure. The resulting cider was being collected in a large vat, to be sold later in 2 litre bottles.

Shortly after he bought the mill, Shafer saw the need for a cider press in the district.

"I looked all over the province for a really old press — the kind that would go with the mill," he said. "There weren't any for sale, but I did manage to get one over in Syracuse while visiting there. And it's become the mainstay of our business."

They don't press the apples during the cider sipping season. They're at it right up until January.

We said we'd be back to do a story about the mill itself when the pressure was off. Meanwhile, we left with some delicious cider made from apples that came from our old orchard.

Tops in Props

❦

Dolores Holliday is a very crafty lady. While sitting at a sewing machine in her Whitby bungalow, she crafts weird and wondrous creations used as props for theatre companies.

She has always had a yen for theatre and about 10 years ago approached the manager of the Whitby Courthouse Theatre to see if she could fit into their productions in some way. They needed a dresser at the time, and she began assisting in that capacity.

But before long the theatre people discovered that Dolores was quite a seamstress. She also teaches power sewing and crafts at a community college. So when they needed a prop that looked like an iguana for *Night of the Iguana*, they asked if she could make one for them. It was a new challenge. Dolores went to the library, got a few ideas for designs and made a very realistic-looking iguana out of foam and fibre. Since then, she has made all sorts of similar props, many of them now sitting around her basement workshop. There's a ferocious-looking dragon's head that was in *The King and I*, a gorilla from *Cabaret*, a talking camel who had a part in *Ali Baba*, to mention just a few.

As time went on, other amateur theatre companies in Central Ontario began calling upon Dolores for props and special effects. She doesn't charge for them and when they have played their parts she brings them home. She likes having them around.

When we were there, she was working on a pig's head to be used in a production of *Foxfire*. She showed us the process of making it from the first sketch, to the patterns and sewing of the pieces, the gluing, and finally, the painting. Usually she has plenty of time to put the props together, but she had to do the dragon's head in 48 hours, which put her under real pressure.

The creations that come from Mrs. Holliday's hobby may, in some cases, be as vital to a theatre production as the actors, dancers or musicians. Yet her efforts go unnoticed by the audience.

"That's the way it's supposed to be," says Dolores. "If I do the job properly, the things I do should just blend into the production on stage."

Meanwhile, she sits at her sewing machine surrounded by her various and diverse critters. They're a motley crew, but they're quiet, easy to get along with, and don't run around the house. Just stay propped up in their proper places.

Shoes for Moos

❧

Don't think you're going bonkers if you happen to see a cow wandering around a farmer's field wearing colourful rubber boots.

It's not a fashion trend. Those boots were made for walking in muddy fields and barnyards. Just the thing for cattle with sore feet.

Jim Wells, a fast-talking, fast-moving grey-haired stocky Scot who runs a work-wear store in the village of Elmira, in Mennonite country, got the germ of the idea from several farmers.

Jim isn't a farmer. He's a salesman, and his sales instincts were triggered as he listened to his farmer-customers complain about their cattle's diseased or injured hooves being infected as they roamed over wet and sloppy patches of ground.

He did some research, and learned there were protective coverings on the market in Europe and Australia, but they were mostly plastic affairs that didn't seem to fill the bill.

Jim thought rubber boots might do the trick. He designed a boot, shaped to a cow's foot, and had a limited number made up at Kaufman Rubber in nearby Kitchener. His farmer friends snapped them up.

As word got around, cattle farmers from beyond the district began phoning in orders. In a few weeks, he had sold about 5,000 units, and Kaufmans had to hire additional staff to keep up with the demand.

Wells realized he had a tiger by the tail. He set up franchises from Vancouver to the Maritimes, and put salesmen on the road.

One of the first of the local farmers to get Jim's new product was Rick Shantz who has a dairy farm a few miles from Elmira.

We went out to the Shantz farm to see "Shoes For Moos" on the hoof, as it were.

We watched as Rick and Jim gave us a demonstration of how

the boots are used. Jim patted a gentle cow named Mary, while Rick lifted up one of her front hooves and put on the black boot. Then he buckled up two yellow straps. The yellow straps are for easy identification when cattle are in the fields.

"The boots are just what we needed," said Rick. "If cattle have hoof rot they may not need medication as long as the hoof can be kept clean and dry for a few days."

Wells was saying the market is unlimited. "There are about 2 million cattle in Canada, and about 11 million in the States," he said. "The U.S. is our next market."

There's no question that both farmers and their cattle will benefit from Jim's idea. And for fashion-conscious cows, "Shoes For Moos" provide the niftiest booties in the barnyard.

The Papa Bear

One of God's great gifts to the world is the teddy bear. I remember my own teddy bear as if it were yesterday. One of his eyes was missing, but he was a cuddly, snuggly little bear and we used to have long talks. He was a consoling friend when things went wrong, especially serious things, like having to go to bed early.

Recently, I met another, larger teddy bear, whose name is Fred Smith. Although he is only one of about a thousand other bears who live in Lee Wansbrough's house in Fergus, when I saw him I had a feeling we had met before. I began to wonder if it could be my own little bear who had grown up.

Anyway, Fred sat beside me on a chesterfield in the Wansbrough living room. I put my arm around him and we sat there and listened as Lee told us about Good Bears of the World, and his latest project, Bears on Patrol, which involves the OPP.

Let me explain all this. Bear with me, as Lee would say.

First of all, Lee Wansbrough is a bear of a man himself. He's built along the lines of a professional football player — not the type you expect to be a teddy bear collector.

He's not just an average collector, either. When he retired because of ill health, teddy bears became his vocation in life. He founded the first Canadian den of Good Bears of the World, an organization with thousands of members who distribute teddy bears to children in hospitals and other places where the small stuffed bears can be a source of comfort.

Lee became an authority on the bears, and his knowledge of the history and varieties of them is extraordinary. He has far-flung contacts with others who share his interest. His wife Judy handles his extensive correspondence and the bookings for the many talks he gives at shows, schools, hospitals and seniors' residences.

His latest project is truly heartwarming. After months of negotiation, he arranged to have the OPP carry teddy bears in their cruisers and boats, so when children are faced with traumatic situations such as accidents or family disputes, the officers have a teddy bear to give them, and it works!

The idea is being financed by individuals, corporate contributions, and especially the Ontario branch of the Telephone Pioneers of America which is made up of active and retired telephone workers.

As I was leaving, I took a last look at Fred Smith. I was still sure I'd seen him before. Who knows? In this mysterious universe, strange things can happen, and if you have a child-like imagination, almost anything can happen.

Billy the Kid

❦

I saw a "magic lantern" recently at a travelling display of early cinema equipment that happened to be at a museum in Huronia. And I was mesmerized by memories.

I had a "magic lantern" just like it when I was a boy. It was my pride and joy. It was a box-like projection that illuminated slides. My "silver screen" was one of my mother's bedsheets.

When I was about nine I became a youthful impresario. I'd put on "shows". The "magic lantern" eventually became involved in my brief career as an impresario, but in the early days I was more inclined toward "live" dramatic productions.

My dramatic offerings usually featured three of my friends who lived in the same block. The shows would be held in our garage. The seats were planks resting on boxes.

I'd get together with my friends to make up the plots. One I remember was about pirates. It had a very bloodthirsty theme. Very often, however, the plot would change in the middle of the performance if one of the actors decided to go in another direction. This didn't bother the case one bit. Boyhood imagination is never structured. We'd just ad lib around it.

I say "boyhood imagination" because girls weren't allowed to participate. In fact we weren't too keen on even having them in the audience. But if they had the one cent admission price we'd tolerate them in the back row.

The most popular drama we ever put on was called *The Ghost of Albany Avenue,* which was the name of the street where most of us lived. My mother's bedsheet came in handy again, this time as the ghost's costume.

But my most successful venture as an impresario centred around the aforementioned "magic lantern".

I planned a showing of slides well in advance — the day

before the event. I painted two paper posters and nailed them to telephone poles in the neighbourhood. The posters read "Big Magic Lantern Show — Bill's Garage". Word got around.

Then I got the show together. I had accumulated about 30 slides. I hung up my mother's bedsheet again. It was a bit dirty by this time since the ghost in the play had let it drag on the garage floor. The admission was two cents for this special occasion, but I figured the show was worth it.

I had cut out several small paper tickets. The next day I sold them at the door. And lo and behold I sold 21 tickets! That's counting the three girls who sat in the back row.

The show consisted of five slides of a "Mutt and Jeff" cartoon and the feature was along National Geographic lines. I provided the commentary. I'd say, "This is an elephant...this one is a mountain." The script was pared to the bone. Nothing fancy. Just the facts.

At the end there was scattered applause, mostly by the girls. The show was a hit.

I decided to run another show the following week, and got my first lesson in merchandising. I raised the price to three cents. Nobody showed up. I had priced myself right out of the market.

Elly's Fame

❦

Corbeil is a typical Northern Ontario village east of North Bay that was in the news over half a century ago as the birthplace of the Dionne Quintuplets.

Today, it's the home of another famous family — the Johnstons. There's Dr. Rod Johnston, his wife Lynn, and their two children. But the millions of people the world over who read about them every day wouldn't recognize them by the name Johnston. They know them as John, Elly, Michael and Lizzy as they follow their humorous and human family escapades in the comic strip "For Better or For Worse".

The cartoonist is Lynn Johnston, "Elly" in the strip that goes to 900 daily and weekly newspapers around the world and is translated into four languages.

The Johnstons live in a beautiful log house in a secluded forest area a few miles from Corbeil. Rod has a dental practice in North Bay and the children go to school nearby. Their famous mother's studio is in the basement of the house, and the walls are covered with the works of other well-known fellow cartoonists.

Jenny and I had met the family in a casual way some years ago. This time when we went back to see them, it was to do a T.V. item and Terry Culvert was with us. He's a cartoonist himself, so he and Lynn had a lot in common and hit it off right away.

As usually, Lynn was swamped with work and obligations of one kind or another. She had just returned from a promotional tour for one of her books of cartoons, and was trying to pick up the pieces.

While we were there, she answered two or three overseas telephone calls regarding an international convention of cartoonists she'd been asked to organize. And when Terry was shooting pictures of her at her easel, she wasn't drawing any old thing for our benefit. Time is too valuable. She was doing a bona fide episode of "For Better or For Worse" that would appear in a couple of months. The strip has to be sent to the distributing syndicate at least six weeks in advance.

Although she's been at the top of the heap in the business for over a decade now, success didn't come easily. Lynn, who was born in Collingwood, moved to Vancouver where she studied art and animation and later did flyers, commercial work and whatnot for years before getting the big break — syndication!

Suddenly, she was sought after as a speaker, panellist, commentator, and guest on network shows in the States. T.V. and film crews discovered the family's retreat and her life was turned topsy-turvey.

Those days have passed. She put her foot down. The interview we had in her home was a rare one. She now confines such things to press conferences when she's travelling.

And how does she look upon fame? Lynn shook her head. "If you let it get to you, it's destructive," she said. "At best, it's just garbage."

As we left, she and Jenny were talking about the real things in life. Such as where to get a bargain in slacks over at a North Bay shopping mall. The sort of thing Elly might talk about in "For Better or For Worse".

Ghost Story

❦

We've been to the southwestern Ontario village of Lucan quite a few times, mostly to do stories about the Donnellys.

They were hard-drinking, fighting, feuding Irish immigrant family that, in the last century, caused all sorts of trouble around the village with their escapades. Eventually, every violent thing that happened in the district was blamed on the Donnellys whether they did it or not.

Then on the night of February 4, 1880, a vigilante group descended on the Donnelly cabin in nearby Biddulph Township and brutally murdered and mutilated five members of the family, including Joanna, the mother.

It was one of the most vicious episodes in the annals of Canadian crime. Some of the vigilantes were brought to trial. It's thought even the town constable was in on it. At any rate, none were convicted and Lucan became known as Canada's most lawless town.

I'd had more than a casual interest in the story because Terry Culbert, our cameraman, was born and raised there and knows all of the historical details.

But recently, there was another development. The son of one of the murdered brothers built a house on the family property some years ago. And late last year a schoolteacher named Robert Salts and his wife Linda bought the house and surrounding property, which includes the original barn, and the cement remnants of the cabin. The interesting thing about it is that Robert Salts is a trance psychic!

I've done stories about psychic phenomena and observed psychics while they're in a trance. There's nothing new about it. Similar principles have been common in the East for thousands of years.

At any rate, Robert says when they moved into the house, his keen perceptions sensed something.

"I felt quite at ease in the house itself," he said. "But out in the barn, I felt I was being watched. This was intensified later and I became aware of figures. There were men with black beards. And I have seen Joanna several times. She wears a dark dress and a bonnet."

Along with that, a friend of ours, Karen Winstone, visited the site after the Salts family moved in. She took a photograph out in the barn. There was a strange luminous light in the picture. The people who developed it checked both the camera and the film. They had no explanation for the strange light.

Since Robert Salts is a recognized psychic with a clientele who come to him for health energy and psychic advice, his perceptual powers cannot be completely dismissed.

It's possible, I suppose, that the restless spirits of the Donnellys still roam the place. In any event, the circumstances add still another chapter to the Donnelly saga. One that seems shrouded in mystery.

Art in Reverse

❧

There are quite a few artists in and around the Town of Simcoe, but none quite like Linda Sanderson. In fact, it's unlikely there's another artist in the whole country that paints just like her.

Linda, who works in a basement studio in her home, paints on glass! It's reverse painting, and it's tricky. She paints on one side of the glass, then flips it over and you see the finished product.

It's an ancient art that dates back to the 12th century, but Linda didn't know that when she began doing it. She hadn't researched the method or studied it. She hit upon it in what she describes as a "fortunate accident".

One day she picked up a piece of glass to use as a temporary palette and noticed the colours on the glass were "brighter, more magical and intense". She discarded traditional ways of painting and began using glass as a "canvas".

Jenny and Terry, both accomplished artists who were interested in the unusual medium, were even more impressed by the paintings themselves. So was I.

They're populated by lots of people. They're whimsical. Some have a childlike quality. Each of the paintings expresses an idea along the lines of Linda's own optimistic cheerful outlook on life, and her bubbling sense of humour.

All of the paintings have titles. "The Birth of the Blues" shows an open egg with jazz musicians playing inside. Others are called "Home Ice", and "Dancing Cheek to Cheek".

Although she's been showing her work at art shows for close to a decade, the attractive mother of two has been known mostly for the medium rather than the message. That is, until last year. Then Sanderson hit the jackpot!

She was chosen to do the poster for the Royal Winter Fair. The prints of the posters sell in the thousands every year. On top of that she was commissioned to do the UNICEF cards which are distributed worldwide. Suddenly she had her first taste of fame and international recognition!

We watched her working on a commission for the Ontario Government. When you're doing reverse glass painting, a lot of detail is involved. Four layers of paint are required. It takes Linda at least six weeks to do a painting, and she manages to turn out about eight a year.

It's hard to describe her work. It's not exactly "folk art". Linda calls it "naive" style. I guess it's just a consistently happy look at the little, ordinary things of life more than anything. One thing I know. Every painting makes you smile.

What Price Decoys

❦

We arrived in Athens one sunny morning in late October. That's not the Athens of the Acropolis and all those irritable ungodly gods that caused the Greeks so much trouble. The Athens I'm talking about is a village of 1,000 people in Eastern Ontario, north of Gananoque. It's known as the first place in Ontario to have huge murals painted on the sides of buildings in the downtown core, which in Athens' case is its tiny main street.

It's also known by many duck hunters as the home of Stephen Lloyd, who has what is likely the largest collection of classic duck decoys in the country.

We'd heard about Lloyd's collection from a hunter we'd met at a Sportsman's Show, and later phoned to ask if we could take a look at his decoys. He said he's be happy to see us.

When we were making an Eastern Ontario swing, we went to his home a couple of miles outside of Athens. He greeted us with youthful enthusiasm. Somehow I'd expected an older man — the gentle, quiet type whose hobby was collecting decoys in his retirement years. But Steve was a tall, lithe, bubbling young man in his mid-40s (anybody under 60 is young to me).

"All the decoys are down in the basement. I have 300 and I've got them all set up for you." The words tumbled out in rapid-fire fashion. He reminded me of a high-pressure magazine salesman I'd once known.

But he knew we weren't there to buy anything. In the first place, the decoys weren't for sale. In the second place, when we went downstairs, some of them, to my untrained eye, looked like the memorable junk I used to see in my Uncle Fred's cluttered attic. Or possibly the kind of thing you might pick up for a dollar or so at a flea market.

I mentioned this to Steve as gently as possible, searching within myself for a few dormant threads of diplomacy.

"You're right on!" he chortled. "I got this beauty for a few dollars 10 years ago. Now it's valued at $500."

I stared at the decrepid-looking duck in disbelief. It was badly worn and had buckshot holes in it. But I'd heard Steve was an expert in the field and often called upon to evaluate decoys at shows and fairs. I decided I'd better keep an open mind.

"Look at the carving on this one," Steve raced on, stroking the duck appreciatively. "It's a George Warin from 1850." He picked up another. "Here's one by Ken Winger. Some of his work is valued at about $25,000. Of course, in the States, people will pay up to $300,000 for a classic carving."

Suddenly my mind was opened! Suddenly I saw the artistry of it all! At those prices, it became obvious that somebody knew a lot more than I did. I took a new look at the weatherbeaten masterpieces as Steve pointed out some of the more intricate designs.

As a going away present, Steve gave me a decoy I had admired. I have no intention of giving it to my youngest grandson to play with in his bath. I think I'll rent a safety deposit box at a bank and deposit my decoy. Then I'll be able to duck into a vault every once in a while, and gaze at my holdings the way rich people do.

Bonhomme's Syrup

At the end of a country road near the Southern Georgian Bay village of Lafontaine is Alcide Ladouceur's place. Nobody ever calls him by his real name. He's known as "Bonhomme" (good man).

Bonhomme is 80 now. He lives alone in a house that once held 20 Ladouceurs. He's short, stubby and jovial. He could be "Doc" of the Seven Dwarfs. But he's not that short, and not as cranky either.

Sheltered in a forest behind his house is an old sugar shack where Bonhomme makes maple syrup as did his great grandfather when he came to this country in the 1700s.

When we were there, the season was just beginning. Some of his 12 living children and a few of his grandchildren were helping him gather the sap from the many pails scattered around among the trees. There was none of the usual plastic tubing connecting the trees you see these days. Bonhomme doesn't like it.

Inside the shack his son "Fritz" (his real name is Wilfred) was stoking the wood-burning stove which heats the evaporators, and the resulting maple syrup was being drained into tins by one of Bonhomme's daughters.

Bonhomme's maple syrup has gone as far afield as the Vatican! He's been to Rome a few times on tours. The last time he packed a tin of syrup and, escorted by a priest friend of his, gave it to one of the Pope's secretaries. He shows me a letter of thanks from the Pope of which he is very proud.

"I don't expect my syrup to be as good this year," said Bonhomme. "The acid rain has something to do with it, but on top of that, God didn't send the right weather."

Nevertheless, when we joined Bonhomme and his children for pancakes which "Fritz" made, the syrup we poured on them tasted excellent. So, despite the acid rain, bad weather and all the rest of it, Bonhomme's maple syrup is still mighty good stuff.

Kings of the Road

❦

You don't see much evidence of brotherly love on busy highways. It's mostly a dot-eat-dog proposition. A survival of the fittest. But every once in a while the gentler side of human nature emerges.

One day when we were driving up toward Thunder Bay, traffic suddenly stopped in both directions. We were about the fourth car back in our line. At first we thought it might be an accident or possible road construction. Then we noticed people in the cars ahead laughing and smiling. A few got out of their cars to see what was going on.

It turned out a mother partridge had decided to lead her brood across the road. She had assumed territorial rights, and neither traffic nor squealing brakes deterred her. We caught a glimpse of her walking majestically across the highway, her five little ones tagging along in single file behind her.

When the small parade had safely reached the other side and disappeared into the bush, the car engines were revved up and the motorists (many of them seasoned veterans of combat zones like Highway 401) moved off again. There was something heartwarming about the episode.

Of course, we've encountered similar things in our travels around the province. One time on the highway leading into Bancroft, traffic was stopped when a black bear lumbered across the road. And it's common to see deer and moose.

But the most spectacular incident happened when we were in Florida. At one of the busiest intersections in Bromard County, a wayward dog out for a midday romp held up traffic for 20 minutes before two motorcycle policemen herded the hound home.

The year-old dog named Freckles had no traffic sense and was running straight at cars. Drivers were swerving and hitting their brakes to avoid him.

With blue lights flashing and sirens wailing, the officers roared to the rescue. But Freckles crossed a median into another lane. Then it took off in the opposite direction. Everything stopped and people got out of their cars to cheer for either the police or the dog, I'm not sure which.

Finally, Freckles ran up the doorsteps of a house. The police caught him and traced the owner, a girl who didn't even know he was missing.

The story made the front page of the Miami Herald.

Cosmic Comics

❦

Collectors are an interesting bunch. You see them at shows where they buy, sell and swap all sorts of items from stamps to antique steering wheels.

There are lots of shops in the big cities catering to various specialities, but recently somebody told me about a small store in St. Thomas that deals in nothing but comic books. So we went down to see it.

The shop is called the "Cosmic Comic Connection" which, when you stop to think about it, is a pretty far out name. On top of that, the little two-room shop is packed with about 25 thousand vintage comic books!

The owner is an affable young guy in his early thirties named John Mills. Like most kids, Mills grabbed his first coloured cartoon book out of curiosity. But as fast as you can Robin and

Batman, he was hooked.

That first 10-cent paperback stirred a collector's passion that today represents a stock of old comic books valued in the thousands. To put an exact price on it would be futile since year after year, even month by month, the value increases.

There's everything there from Donald Duck to Superman, but the big sellers today are books featuring horror, war and violence.

"In a way, the books reflect a part of modern history," says Mills. "When comic books first appeared on the market about 50 years ago, they were mostly humorous. Then they evolved into action heroes, and today, the more violent they are the better they sell. It's unfortunate, but that's the way it is."

Youngsters pay a dollar or more these days to read their favourite comics, says Mills. The most popular are X-Men, Punisher and Wolverine books.

But John deals mainly in rare copies with prices usually ranging from $4 to $300, depending on the condition.

He has one copy that's really rare. It's the second appearance of Spiderman issued in 1962. The price? A cool $1,000!

While we were there, a 13-year-old named Marty Gebel and his father came in. Marty had one destination. He found the Spiderman file and started to leaf through it. A few minutes later he triumphantly pulled out a book. "I found one," he shouted to his dad. I asked him why he was so pleased.

"I'm a Spiderman collector," he grinned. "I have 136 different ones so far and this is the 137th."

Later, I asked John if the boy was a regular customer. "No, I've never seen him before," he said. "But I guess he's a born collector, and he's started a hobby that may last a life time. He may branch out to stamps or coins later on. Or maybe something more offbeat. I know one guy about my age who collects antique toilet seats."

Country Club

❦

There's a country club on the outskirts of the village of Bonfield, east of North Bay, that's the only one of its kind I've ever heard of. It's not for people. It's only for dogs and cats!

Technically, I suppose it's a boarding kennel. But it bears no resemblance to one. It looks like a big bungalow set in amongst the northern pines. And, as you come upon it along a winding road, there's a sign reading "Countryside Animal Inn".

Driving up to the house and barn, you see dogs and cats peering out at you from a picture window. You get the feeling they're smiling at you. They look like a happy bunch.

There's a reason for that. They're there on holidays. When you enter, they greet you enthusiastically, but not a snarl to be heard. It appears that they all live there.

There were about twenty in the living room when we arrived. After the greeting, they settled down in their favourite places. Some on chesterfields, others on chairs. They're guests at the club and they have the run of the place!

Mind you, they're very cooperative when the innkeepers Lilo and Bernie Garich ask them to do something like move over to give visitors a chance to sit down. But Lilo and Bernie make it a request rather than a command.

The couple started the club just a few years ago. "We had two dogs and two cats of our own," explains Lilo. "Friends would occasionally leave their pets with us when they went away. Then friends of our friends began to ask us, and eventually we thought we might just as well go into business."

At times, there are up to fifty dogs and cats at the club. Most are regular guests who have met before and are happy to do things together.

We watched them bounding out the back door into a fenced-off play area. They ran around and made lots of noise cavorting in the crisp northern air.

Mealtime is a busy time for Lilo. Each dog has his own bowl and favourite food. The cats sit up on the big kitchen table where Lilo dishes out the goodies and they wait patiently for their snacks.

While we were there, Christine Whatmore, a teacher from North Bay, arrived with her dog Max, a big German Shepherd.

"Max just loves it here," she told us. "He seems to pout a bit when we come to take him home." There's nothing fancy about Countryside. But it has a style of its own. The guests have all the conveniences of home, plus the usual tender loving care they're used to.

Besides, it's nice to get away from it all occasionally. Nice to meet old buddies once again in an easy-going, casual country setting.

Tin for Tole

Robert Faulkner is a tinsmith. He's been a tinsmith since he was 14, when he learned the trade from his father, who learned it from his father.

These days, Robert concentrates his talents on making coffee pots of tin in his workshop on the shores of a lake near Picton.

That doesn't sound very challenging for a man with Faulkner's artistic bent. But these are not ordinary run-of-the-mill coffee pots.

They're heirloom reproductions of originals made by early settlers which are now treasured by museums and private collectors all across the continent.

The limited edition reproductions are ordered by "tole"

painters in both Canada and the United States. That word "tole" is french for decorative painting. The final products are heritage coffee pots bearing magnificent multi-coloured designs.

I watched Faulkner cutting and rounding tin on machines similar to those he used a half-century ago when he worked with his father in England. He found the old machinery at auctions.

He started making the coffee pots about ten years ago when his wife, Eileen, who did tole painting as a hobby, asked him to make something out of tin she could paint.

He made a few things, and in the process, became interested in the historical background of Early American tinware. He also discovered that tinsmiths who made classic reproductions were in great demand.

Robert and Eileen began travelling the continent to study originals at museums and in private collections. Curators were fussy, and it was necessary to wear white gloves to take exact measurements of the valued heritage artifacts.

Tole painters wanted coffee pots more than anything else. Robert took the measurements back to his workshop. He cut patterns and made his first authentic reproductions.

Word got around. Famous tole painters heard about his work. Almost overnight he had more orders than he could handle.

These days, Eileen has little time to do any painting. She's too busy handling correspondence, shipping and business details for what the couple call "Heirloom Reproductions".

It's ironic that Robert would likely never have thought have making the reproductions if his wife hadn't asked for something she could paint.

Now they're both into it up to their necks, with Faulkner an internationally recognized tinsmith.

Marie's Roots

❦

The Georgian Bay village of Lafontaine is a little bit of old Quebec smack in the middle of Ontario. Marie Brunelle has lived there most of her life. She's an Indian woman who was adopted in childhood by a Lafontaine Francophone family and grew up knowing nothing of her native culture.

You may have met her without knowing it. These days, during the summer months, Marie, dressed in her native costume, is on the site at Ste. Marie Among the Hurons. That's the famed reconstruction of Ontario's first European community built in the 17th century. It's only coincidence that she's there at all.

Eight years ago, when she was touring Ste. Marie with her children, she noticed that there were costumed priests, woodmen, carpenters, a blacksmith and so on, but there wasn't a single Indian, although historically Hurons made up a good proportion of the population of the community.

She mentioned this to the directors. She sent letters and made phone calls. They saw her point and asked her if she'd like to be an interpreter of native lore. She told them she knew nothing about Indian ways, having been brought up by a French family. Nevertheless, they sent her up to observe Old Fort William at Thunder Bay, where there's a huge reconstruction of one of the early fortresses with an "Indian Village" just outside the palisades.

"It was there," says Marie, "that I became an Indian. I met an old Indian woman who taught me leather work and other crafts. But more than that, she taught me about my ancestors, taught me to respect nature, taught me to go out in the bush and find the bark and the roots I needed, and to show respect for the spirit of the trees."

Later, Marie was appointed coordinator of the native program at Ste. Marie. At times, her children were with her on the site. She has taught them the other side of their family heritage which she herself had never known as a child.

Marie will be back again at Ste. Marie this summer. Since her first visit as a casual visitor just eight years ago, she has read early Canadian history, learned additional crafts and Indian lore, and has become something of an authority on the ways and beliefs of their forefathers.

Decorative Dobbins

❦

Those prancing, bobbing, merry-go-round horses that sparked our imaginations in childhood aren't confined to carousels anymore.

At the St. Thomas studio of Elisabeth Grieve, we watched craftspeople transforming bare moulded plastic horses into colourful creatures of many hues and sparkling designs.

They weren't destined to go round and round at carnivals and parks. They were going to 400 stores across the country to be sold as gifts or decorative pieces in homes and office buildings!

Elisabeth (it's a Dutch spelling of the name) is a go-getting grandmother who's been a crafts and wreath designer for decades. But a couple of years ago she spotted a developing trend and branched out into the carousel horse business. And it's strictly for the carriage trade, believe me. Some of those horses retail in the thousands!

There's a reason for that. It takes hours before the finished product is ready to hit the road. Three coats of paint are required. Then a coat of blue and another coat of paint. When the blue dries. the paint cracks, giving it an antique look.

Gold leaf is used to finish the horses' manes and tails. Painting the body with designs involves up to 14 different colours.

While we were there, Elisabeth's husband Bill came in to pick up some horses for delivery. Bill is a retired real estate executive who has always supported his wife's various crafty enterprises. He told me a customer once called Elisabeth to say she should fire the delivery man because he was so grouchy.

"Don't let him kid you," laughed Elisabeth. "He's the best sales and public relations type you could find anywhere."

Elisabeth has been on the entrepreneurial merry-go-round for years, and finally caught the brass ring with the carousel idea. A full-sized horse can cost up to $4,000. And with prices like that, there are few people who would look a gift horse in the mouth.

The Great Elm

❦

When historic trees around the province are ready to leave their hallowed places, you'll likely find Jim Judd there as the chainsaws begin their grizzly task.

Jim doesn't cut the trees. He's there to get the wood and take it back to his workshop in Waterford so he can start the old trees on a new career.

Jim and his son Len are expert craftsmen in wood, and the furniture they make out of the ancient trees would knock your eyes out.

Jim was at the McMaster University campus November 19, 1973, when a tree with gnarled limbs silhouetted against a leaden sky waited with dignity for the end. It was a victim of Dutch Elm disease.

The Old Girl had been a grown elm when Wolfe and Montcalm met on the Plains of Abraham. She had been growing when Canada became a nation.

She was always known as The Great Elm by the hundreds of

McMaster students she had shaded. It was said the tree was about 400 years old. She was 80 feet high and 5 feet across at the base of her massive trunk.

Jim had bought the tree from McMaster and after the felling ceremony had the chunks of The Great Elm carted to her new home in Waterford, a village south of Brantford.

Today, slices from that massive trunk are gleaming tables in homes and offices across the country.

In 1975, Judd was on hand in Simcoe when another historic tree inflicted with Dutch Elm disease was brought down. It was 6 feet in diameter.

Jim made a coffee table for his own home out of one of the big slices of wood from the tree's trunk. His dining room table is made of wood that has musket shot embedded in the surface. The wood came from a tree that was in a battle zone during the war of 1812.

The furniture the Judds make has a very distinctive quality. They use a heavy protective resin coating that seals against moisture and strengthens the wood while enhancing the grain.

Jim is retiring gradually from furniture making. Len does most of the actual work these days. But his dad still keeps his eyes open for old trees that Len can turn into fine new furniture.

Old Dance Hall

❧

There's an old dance hall called "Play Time" in Warminster, just south of London. It's closed now, but the owner, Frank Susko, left it just the way it was in its glory years. The decorations are still intact, and these days it has an additional role. It acts as a shrine of sorts. It houses Susko's collection of musical memorabilia. There are musical instruments and records, but most surprising of all is an amazing collection of sheet music. Believe it or not, Frank has accumulated over 10,000 pieces of sheet music!

Tables have been set up on part of the dance floor and some of the sheet music is spread out on them. Many of the songs go back to the turn of the century. Almost all were published at least 50 or 60 years ago. I remembered some I heard in childhood like "Peggy O'Neil" and "When You and I Were Young Maggie". And I have fond memories of "Thanks For the Buggy Ride" and "Ramona". But "The Bird on Nellie's Hat" was new to me. Of course, it came out in 1916, when I was just a year old.

I'd assumed Frank had picked up much of the music from other collectors, but he told me that this wasn't the case. "I don't know of any other collectors," he said, "not on this scale, anyway. Some have a few pieces of music among their old records, but as far as I know, this is the biggest private collection anywhere. I get them from garage sales, flea markets, anywhere I happen to find them."

Not all of the instruments and sheet music are at the dance hall. Some of them Frank keeps at his home on Valley Street in nearby Port Stanley. In one section of the living room there are records and music piled up to the ceiling.

Frank is a 76-year-old retired farmer and part-time musician who still plays the banjo. In the winter he and his wife go south where he plays with a senior's band in Sarasota.

Along with the memorabilia, "Play Time" has always been just a hobby with Frank. He doesn't intend to change the dance hall. There are old 78 records and posters hanging on the walls, crystal balls hanging from the ceiling, and the bandstand hasn't been altered a bit. The instruments and music stands are still there, and you expect the musicians to return at any moment to play another set.

It reminded me of the typical dance halls of yesteryear. It's a nostalgic place. The songs may have ended, but the melodies still remain.

Curling Club

❦

If I ever saw a bunch of fun-loving kids, it's the old-timers of Minden Seniors Curling Club. It's no ordinary curling club. With a membership of over 200, it's thought to be the largest club of its kind in the province!

Since Minden itself has a population of only about 1,200, some of the members come from the many nearby communities which are nestled in the valleys of the Haliburton Highlands.

The whole area is dotted with lakes, streams, cottages and cabins, and ideal for both summer and winter sports. Minden is especially noted for its Sled Dog Derby. But I didn't know about the curling club until one day, when I was sitting in a restaurant in Haliburton, a vibrant white-haired lady named Alberta Maitland came over and told me about it. She was bubbling with enthusiasm.

A few days later, I happened to be in Minden and dropped into the curling club. Alberta had good reason to be enthusiastic. There were well over a hundred seniors milling about at the time. Some were out on the ice, others were sitting around the big lounge overlooking the rink. They were talking, laughing and kidding one another.

Alberta was there and introduced me to some of them. At least 10 members of the club were in their 80s. I watched a sprightly-looking man down on the rink throwing a rock, then gracefully sliding along the ice behind it.

"That's Jack Gregory," said Alberta. "He'll be 89 pretty soon." I stared in disbelief. He appeared to be 60 at the most. Later, I met 86-year-old Pat Clarke, and 82-year-old Ed Pettinger who was the club's first president when it was started 20 years ago. "We found the competition with the juniors too tough," said Ed, "and decided to form our own club. And besides, they take the game too seriously. We just like to have some fun."

The youngest member is a woman. She's only 59, but they let her join anyway. She's the kid.

Fall Fair

❦

I get to at least one Fall Fair every year. I never get tired of them. In recent years, I visited fairs in Caledon, Cobalt, Elmvale, Orillia and so forth, finishing off the season at the Royal Winter Fair.

One year I dropped around to the Norfolk County Fair in Simcoe, and before that to the fair in the village of Coldwater. The Simcoe fair has become quite an event. That year there were about 175,000 people in attendance. It's become quite large. I thoroughly enjoyed it, but I still have a soft spot in my heart for the little fellas.

The attendance at the Coldwater Fair, for example, hasn't fluctuated much for decades. It's still small. But it's the real thing. You catch the country spirit as you begin to wander around. The fair seems to express the soul of Ontario's rural life. It seems to express the deep devotion to the land that has characterized farmers and their families throughout the annals of agricultural life in the province.

I went to the fair's office in the arena. The secretary-treasurer, Cherryll Barr, had a baby in one arm and a telephone receiver tucked on the shoulder of the other. Calls were coming in thick and fast. She handles them calmly. She knew all the answers. She took time out to introduce me to a few of the veteran fair-goers. They all had farm backgrounds. Even their names had a rural ring. Maggie Furs told me she had 100 vegetable entries. She'd been coming to the fair since she was a girl. She was 80 at the time. And I met Ethyl Fagan, who'd been showing maple syrup, crafts and knitting for 60 consecutive years. Another veteran was Cyril Martin. He was 84. He said he'd been going to the fair since the tender age of two.

"It's bigger than it was in the early days," said Cyril, "Mostly because of the arena. But the grounds are about the same."

I looked over at the heavy horses, the 4-H members and their calves. The regular things you find at most fairs. I can't quite put my finger on why that little fair has such a special appeal. Perhaps it's because it's unpretentious. It hasn't succumbed to technological gimmicks to satisfy modern tastes and demands. The people who attend it and the people who run it seem totally unconcerned about that double-edged term called "progress".

Lafleur Gardens

❦

I've met interesting people and seen interesting places during our visits to Northern Ontario. The splendour of Lake Superior's north shore is etched in my memory. Joining my prospector buddy Alex Peron as we trudged through the bush to his mining camp one autumn morning brings happy recollections.

But one of the most surprising places we've visited is a huge gardening complex in Timmins called Lafleur Gardens. Somehow, you don't expect to see such a showplace in a mining town. On top of that, it was originally started by an underground miner and his wife, and now their seven sons and their wives are in the business.

Back in 1946, Agnas Lafleur and his wife Germaine planted a vegetable garden, primarily for their own use. But before long, they were selling their surplus produce at the local Farmer's Market. When the market closed in the mid '60s, they converted an old garage into a vegetable stand. Later, their sons built a small greenhouse out of old windows for them, which was heated with a coal oil furnace. The greenhouse was filled with tomatoes and bedding plants. The first crop was a sellout and a second greenhouse was built the following year. It continued that way year after year throughout the '70s until there were thousands upon thousands of square feet of greenhouses.

As the business grew, all seven of the Lafleurs' sons became involved in it. Marcel was put in charge of a Garden Centre. It's become a magnificently colourful place where bridal couples often go to have their wedding pictures taken.

Shortly after, brothers Richard and Robert started a landscaping division serving Northern Ontario. A nursery stock division was added, and then a forestry division which I found the most impressive of all.

In vast greenhouses, the Lafleurs grow 12 million small trees a year. They are supplied to the Ministry of Natural Resources and companies such as E. B. Eddy for their reforestation projects. When you walk into the greenhouses, the tree seedlings extend as far as the eye can see.

Agnas and Germaine are now crowding 80, but are still on the job every day. Meanwhile, that little vegetable garden they started has become a multi-million dollar business.

Planes in Bottles

❧

Doug Painter has been fascinated by airplanes since he was just a tad of a lad growing up in Gloucestershire, England. When other kids were playing soccer, Doug was hanging around the hangars at a nearby airfield watching planes soar into the wild blue yonder. Later, he learned to fly, was employed at an aircraft company and ultimately became a pilot with the Royal Air Force.

Today, the retired North York resident's interest in planes is as keen as ever, although it has taken a different twist. He makes classic model planes. Nothing too unusual about that. But Doug's planes are in bottles!

That's right. He builds the planes mostly from plywood or plastic. Then he takes them apart piece by piece, inserts them through the neck of the bottle using long, thin pliers, then gingerly glues them together. It's an amazing thing to watch.

Painter is thought to be the only person anywhere who can achieve this complex feat. It was enough for Ripley's "Believe It or Not" to award him a certificate, and feature his work in one of their syndicated cartoons which go to hundreds of newspapers the world over.

Doug seems to take it all in stride. A small, wiry, vibrant man in his seventies, he seems unconcerned about the many awards he has received for his work. But he bubbles with enthusiasm as he tells you about the background of each plane which he has researched with meticulous care.

In one old prune juice jug, he's assembled a brief history of aircraft. He's crammed models of the Wright Brothers' Kittyhawk, a sleek Concorde and a space shuttle! In another bottle is one of Canada's famed Snowbirds, and a Red Arrow from the British Aerobatic team. In another is a "wing-walker" standing atop an old biplane. The kind of thing you used to see when "barnstormers" would perform at fairs.

In the past decade Painter has bottled over 200 of the little planes. His North York apartment is chock full of them. It takes weeks, even months, to complete a single model.

"The biggest problem," says Doug, "is finding the right bottles. The next is finding the patience to stay with it. When you're in there, you can't rush or you'll ruin the whole show."

He says he's like to teach the craft to someone, but when people see what's involved they back away from it. "I can't say I blame them. Only an idiot like myself would try it," he laughs.

Far from being an idiot, Painter is a highly skilled craftsman with a flair for the unique. Just ask the man from Ripley's.

Bob's Critters

❦

Artist Bob Short likes to putter around in garbage dumps. There are two dumps on the outskirts of the village of Haliburton where he lives, and Bob visits them about three times a week. It may seem a strange way for an artist to spend his time, but there's a good reason for it.

During these forays into the realm of what most of us consider junk, Bob salvages nuts, bolts, pieces of wood and a variety of disintegrating remnants of old farm machinery. He carts them off to his workshop cabin on the shores of nearby Maple Lake and then unleashes his creative imagination.

The result is what he calls his "critters". He assembles the ancient pieces of wood and metal into weird and wondrous art forms. They may become forest animals, birds, fish, or even strange-looking people. He doesn't sculpt them. He just assembles the things with simple tools.

We watched Bob as he was putting together what he said was going to be a northern eagle. Its eventual destination was Toronto's Northern Secondary School, where Short was an art teacher until his retirement. Later, we went over to the Rail's End Gallery in Haliburton which is in a converted railroad station. They were featuring a showing of Bob's work.

About 20 of his pieces were set up in one of the large rooms. Short's lively sense of humour shone through in both the works themselves and the titles which were attached. For example, "Altered Genes" was the title given to a two-foot-high ostrich that had laid four eggs. Three of the eggs were brass casters which had likely come from old bedposts. But the fourth egg was an ordinary baseball. "That's what happens when you alter genes," chuckled Bob.

Three figures representing the clergy were entitled "Brother

Erroneous", "Sister Ironica" and "Father Axel". The critter that impressed cameraman Terry the most was "Hedge-hog". Its body appeared to be the face of an old clock.

When Bob begins to assemble the pins, screws, wheels and whatnot, he doesn't work within a set boundary. "I don't say that today I'm going to make a bird or something," he says. "If I see an article that suggests something, then I start to build."

When we were at the gallery, almost half of Bob's critters had been sold. It's not just his imaginative skill that attracts people, it's his humorous approach to his creations that's so appealing. by the way, he called his show "The Boy From Ogg". Ogg standing for "Outer Garbage Galaxy".

Creative Powers

❦

When I was very young I started a butterfly collection. As I recall, I also began a stamp collection and a coin collection. None of them ever amounted to much. I guess I just didn't have the knack. John G. Powers did. By the time he was 13, the National Geographic had done a story about his butterfly collection. Today he has a collection of 20,000 of the beautiful creatures and is known internationally as "The Butterfly Man".

His cottage-like home in Cambridge bulges with butterflies. There are species and varieties from all over the world. Among them is the world's largest owlet moth. With a wingspan of 12.16 inches, it's in the Guiness Book of Records. There are hundreds of exotic-looking butterflies carefully framed and preserved which are set up in the living room of the house. Most are from faraway places, but some are native to Canada, like the tiger moth and the tiger swallowtail, neither of which I'd seen before.

Powers, now in his early 40s, is a former teacher and

policeman who chucked it all a few years ago to make his lifelong hobby a business which he calls "Flying Jewels". It's a business that keeps him flying in all directions.

But that's not all. Aside from the butterflies, Powers also has a massive collection of bugs. There are good bugs, bad bugs, giants of the bug world. The unusual, the deadly, even the beautiful. They make up a travelling educational show. Ironically, it's sponsored by the makers of the bug spray Raid. As a result of this enterprise, Powers is known in some circles as "The Bug Man".

On top of it all, Powers has another company known as "Creative Powers". Having been blessed with a creative mind, John comes up with all sorts of advertising and promotional ideas, mostly tied in with butterflies and bugs. His clients include companies large and small. He has 16 registered trademarks and has supplied ideas for 80 products.

In his basement there's an assortment of files, specimens, framed samples, glass jars of all sizes and incoming mail on every bench, table and desk. As he shows you around, John positively bristles with vitality. He talks with a machine-gun delivery as he reaches down into his reservoir of ideas that have immediate appeal.

Powers is a versatile entrepreneur whose every waking moment is taken up with butterflies, bugs and a mind constantly whirling around with — what else? — Creative Powers!

Foxy Pair

❦

This Fox and the Pheasant Lady are the most colourful pair I've met in some time.

Their real names are Doug and Deborah McKinley. Doug is a businessman — an entrepreneur. Deborah is a former fashion consultant. A couple of years ago they decided to get away from it all and move to the country. But they did it with flair.

They bought a magnificent old home in Pine River Valley south of Collingwood. It's set on top of a hill overlooking the valley, and the view is one of grandeur. You get the feeling that on a clear day you could see the whole province!

They're flamboyant people. Live with zest. I'd seen both of them on television. Doug does commercials for one of his automobile franchises called Foxhill. He comes on strong. He's a big man with long white hair and a flowing beard. He looks like a cross between Santa Claus and Ernest Hemingway, and has a driving rasping voice. For years, his friends have called him the Silver Fox, which has eventually abbreviated into just The Fox.

Deborah has appeared many times on Global's News at Noon as a fashion expert. She's a tall, glamorous beauty, considerably younger than Fox.

When they moved to the country, they had no intention of returning to a pioneer lifestyle or anything like that. They brought their extensive collection of antiques and furnished the house luxuriously.

The Fox also brought along his yacht, and it's moored in a small man-made pond just down from the house. He had it set there by derrick.

"I'll take you on a cruise to nowhere," booms the Fox. He's not kidding. The pond is only about 150 yards long and there's not even room to turn the yacht around. But it makes a great guest house.

Needless to say, they call the Estate "Foxhill". There are a few horses loafing around, and a few sheep. But there are thousands of pheasants.

That's Deborah's new career — raising pheasants. She started with just ten pheasants. Now they're all over the place. Even the pheasant raising is done with a certain flair.

The nursery where the eggs are hatched has a sign outside saying "kindergarten", and other signs designating "Junior School" right up to the university graduates.

As a result of this profitable enterprise, Deborah has become known as The Pheasant Lady.

The Fox and The Pheasant Lady are a vibrant, creative couple who love life. And you get the impression that they've only just begun as they tell you their schemes and dreams for their beloved Foxhill.

Guard Donkeys

🍂

If Little Bo-Peep had known a few things about donkeys, she wouldn't have had all that trouble with her sheep.

If seems that donkeys are a sheep's best friend when it comes to keeping the wolf from the flock. Wolves are afraid to tangle with donkeys, as are dogs and other predators.

Gary and Lynn Fox, who have a farm down near Picton in their Bay of Quinte district, have nine donkeys which mingle with their 400-odd sheep. The donkeys don't herd sheep the way sheep dogs do. They're merely on patrol. They just stand around or wander about if they feel like it. A wolf or a dog won't take a chance on getting kicked in the chops. They stay far, far away from those clobbering hooves.

Ever since the donkeys arrived on the scene, the Fox family hasn't lost a single sheep to predators. Before the donkeys came, they were losing up to 20 a year.

Not only that, the donkeys and the sheep have become great buddies. We watched then nuzzling one another out in a field on part of the family's 1,400 acre spread.

Gary and Lynn have been into mixed farming and dairy cattle for years, as were their fathers before them. They also have a few horses.

"I've been around horses all my life," says Gary, "and there's no comparison between a donkey and a horse for fun and friendship. Donkeys are a lot more affectionate."

His favourite is a dark grey donkey called "Blackjack". Gary called out to him and he came trotting over toward us, uttering the familiar hee-haw which Jenny thought sounded like "a rusty barn door."

Gary patted his neck and Blackjack looked at Terry's camera with curiosity. Finally, he walked over and tried to nibble at the lens. Terry chuckled and quickly moved to a new location.

After Terry got the shots he needed, we stayed around for awhile to watch the donkeys and the sheep at play. "You can watch them for hours," smiled Lynn. "They're always doing something interesting."

The Fox family feels a lot more secure with the donkeys out in the fields. And the sheep? Well, with their donkey friends around, who's afraid of the big bad wolf?

Bandura Revival

❦

We meet all sorts of creative people in our travels around the province, and the variety of their interests seems endless.

For example, in the basement workshop of his Oshawa home, Bill Vetzel makes traditional Ukrainian musical instruments known as banduras. And he's the only person in the country to make them.

A bandura looks like a cross between a mandolin and a guitar, but has up to 60 strings and, when played, sounds something like a harp.

Making the instruments has become an absorbing hobby with Vetzel, a tool and die maker by trade, and a precision inspector at General Motors.

Now 46, he's been creative since youth. He has some sculpture he did when he was 16, some historical guns and small cannon he crafted later and, more recently, the Ukrainian musical instruments.

Of Ukrainian background, he became especially interested in the bandura, and discovered that the classical musicians who play the instrument had to get them from the handful of craftsmen in the States who make them.

He began a study of the instrument, including the historical background and building methods used by craftsmen over the years. He constructed the specialized machinery he would need, and began turning out banduras.

We watched as he hollowed out a base. He uses maple, willow, basswood or mahogany. On another machine, he carved out a top made of spruce. Later, he showed us how he made his own strings. While he worked, he told us something about the origins of the instrument.

"Centuries ago," he said, "the bandura was a communications link between the villages. Wandering minstrels roved the countryside playing and singing ballads of hope or sadness and, at times, messages."

Vetzel had arranged to have Yarko Antonevych, a young professional classical bandurist, play for us while we were visiting. We listened as his fingers flew across the strings creating beautiful melodies.

Bill Vetzel watched him with pride and admiration. Pride, because the instrument he had made produced such sounds. Admiration, because despite repeated attempts, Vetzel has never been able to learn to play a bandura.

Nothing too unusual about that. Apparently, Stradivari couldn't play the violin either.

Pick Your Own

❦

When Adrien Gervais bought 350 acres of land north of Barrie in 1968, he bought it as an operating tobacco farm with the possibility of growing fruit in the future.

He had spent six months looking for the right type of land. He wanted elevation and sandy-loam soil. Barrie Hill Farms, as it was known, seemed to fill the bill. Adrien was an experienced farmer who had moved from Quebec. He operated the property as a tobacco farm for a while, then began to raise strawberries, selling them on a pick-your-own basis. The idea was fairly new at the time.

He had no trouble selling them, so he added raspberries and asparagus as additional crops. Then he planted 500 blueberry plants which he bought in Michigan.

The whole thing caught on, and these days up to a thousand people a day visit the farm during the blueberry season alone. We usually go there in the latter part of August. The big parking lot is always jammed, and busloads of people from the city are coming and going. Adrien and his wife Evelyn oversee the arrivals and departures. In many cases, the couple greet the customers like old friends at a reunion. There are handshakes and slaps on the back. They're mostly city people who come back year after year.

There are no professional pickers employed. They aren't needed. But there's a staff to take care of the equipment and to take people out to the fields in carts to pick their own. I guess Barrie Hill Farms has become one of the largest of its kind in the province. The only other one I've seen of comparable size is down at St. Williams, west of Simcoe.

As a rather novel twist, little stools are provided out in the berry patches to make the job of picking considerably easier.

The big blue berries they grow are of three varieties — Blue

Bell, Northland and Blue Jays. They're of excellent quality and Adrien says it's mainly because of the soil.

"I spent months searching southern Ontario before I found exactly what I wanted right here," says Adrien. "The sandy-loam soil suits the berries perfectly and the elevation above the valley saves us from late frosts at the beginning of the season and early fall frosts."

Adrien sees nothing but blue skies for the future of the pick-your-own business. He says that by not having professional pickers he loses some of his crop. On the other hand, when you're getting 120,000 quarts of blueberries a year, such losses are just a drop in the basket.

Pickled Pumpkin

❦

Every year about the middle of October, Marge Schneider begins making pickled pumpkin. I suppose a lot of people do quite a bit of canning during the pumpkin season. But not on the scale Marge does. She uses two and one-half tons of pumpkins!

She doesn't operate a canning factory. She does this on her own with a little help from her friend Laverne Wilson, who cuts the pumpkins into small squares. They work 10 hours a day, four days a week for a month. And they end up with 450 gallon jars of pickled pumpkin!

Marge gets the pumpkin from farmer Tom Haskett's big patch on Highway 24 near Simcoe. Tom carts a number of loads to Marge's "canning cottage" a few miles down the road, and leaves them on the patio in front of the cottage. When we were there, about 300 were patiently sitting on the patio waiting to fulfil their destiny in life.

Inside, Laverne was standing at a table in the kitchen. She was peeling, cutting and dropping the pieces of pumpkin into pails. She worked with the fluid ease of an old pro at the game. After all, she's been helping Marge with the project for the past 25 years.

Marge picked up one of the pails filled with the chunks of pumpkin and dumped them into a batch of boiling syrup on the kitchen stove. Overall, the syrup that's needed requires 40 bales of sugar, two pails of white clover, 150 gallons of vinegar and three pails of crystallized ginger. The pickled pumpkin then went into the gallon jars which were placed in packing cases. The cases were piled almost to the ceiling in an adjoining room. By the way, on top of all this, Marge cans 500 jars of mushrooms, strawberry, raspberry and peach jams every year!

Since the average family requires a fraction of such a volume of preserves, what's the point of Marge making such vast quantities? Well, it all goes to the family's Erie Beach Hotel in nearby Port Dover, which Marge and her husband bought in 1946 and is now operated by their son Tony, along with his other interests. Another son, Bruce, and grandson Andrew are also involved in the business.

The Erie Beach Hotel is an old haunt of ours and one of our favourite inns as we ramble around the province. We always stay in Room 12, which overlooks Port Dover's snug harbour and lighthouse on the pier. And, of course, we often dine at the hotel.

The dining rooms are famous. One of the features on the salad trays are Marge's pickled pumpkins which are gobbled up by about 100,000 diners annually. To Marge, it's a labour of love. To the guests, the pumpkin delicacies are a taste-tempting tradition. And although the Erie Beach is known far and wide for its excellent fish dinners, things just wouldn't be the same without the addition of Marge Schneider's pickled pumpkin.

The Freeloaders

❦

Bugs are interesting things. Children seem fascinated by them. They become totally absorbed in the antics of a bug. As I recall my own favourite was the ladybug, with caterpillars a close second.

I still like to watch bugs. But after so many years of bug watching, I regard them in a completely different way than I did in childhood. I'm no longer so curious about their appearance. My interest in them is now of a more philosophical nature.

While sitting by the kitchen window overlooking the blue waters of Southern Georgian Bay, I may see the occasional ant that has inadvertently arrived on the window sill. I'm sure the ant doesn't want to be there. It will scamper around in all directions trying to figure a way out of the mess it's in.

If I should kill the ant I would likely be doing it a favour. On the other hand, who am I to interfere with the balance of nature? But if Jenny happens to walk by, the problem is solved in one fell swoop. The ant's life span is quickly terminated.

Where caterpillars are concerned, I now take a far more pragmatic approach to the situation. I have seen the damage done to our woodlot by tent caterpillars and more recently by the gypsy moth.

As members of the landowners' reforestation program, our woodlot is managed by the Ministry of Natural Resources. They plant young trees and take care of the nature part of what our grandchildren call "The Green Forest".

In an annual inspection, M.N.R. forester Richard Post found we were being invaded by the dreaded gypsies.

"You've got a problem," said Richard. "Gypsy moths have moved in and we'd better do something about it." It was my first direct encounter with the free-loading travellers that have plagued Ontario trees in the last few years. Richard told me that a single gypsy caterpillar can devour several leaves a day. He pointed out some fuzzy buff-coloured masses on the big maple tree that shades our farmhouse.

"There are the eggs," he said. "They develop into caterpillars which become moths. The females can't fly and lay their eggs wherever they happen to land when blown by the wind. It could be on a boat, truck or tent. That's how they spread to other areas."

In the next half hour I was given a concise outline of what the moths are all about and the sprays to use to get rid of them.

As a result of all this, I now have no compunction about eliminating the creepy crawling caterpillars. They're detrimental hitch-hikers. And as I scraped the gypsy's eggs off our big maple tree on the front lawn, its leaves seemed to gently flutter in a grateful sigh of relief.

Wondrous Wawa

❧

If you travel the Trans Canada Highway along Lake Superior's north shore, you see some of Ontario's most spectacular scenery. The majestic hills, the steep rock cuts and the rivers and streams are visions of rugged beauty.

On the edge of the highway, about a hundred miles west of Sault Ste. Marie, is a massive sculpture of a Canada Goose. It's 28 feet high with a wingspan of 19 feet, and identifies the town of Wawa which in Ojibway means "Wild Goose".

Wawa has become the hub of tourism in the district where the Michipicoten and Magpie Rivers meet. Salmon, walleye, trout and other game fish abound in the waters, and tourists and sportsmen come from all parts of the continent to experience the beauty and attractions of a superb northern vacation land.

We've stopped there a few times for brief visits, but the last time I got caught up in the history of the area and we stayed for a week. This was largely because of Donnie Cheslock, a young dynamo who's a publicist for Michipicoten Township. Donnie hauled out a battered suitcase full of old pictures, drawings and papers about the area's early history. As we sifted through them, I found a drawing of a trading post that had been established back in 1739. It looked like an old fort of some sort.

"It was a centre where the voyageurs could bring their furs," said Donnie. "It's disappeared of course, but I can show you something almost as good."

We took Donnie's panel truck and drove a few miles along winding roads into bush country. Suddenly we came upon a bog ramshackle structure surrounded by palisades of logs that looked surprisingly similar to the drawing I'd seen. There was a large courtyard, a lookout tower, a small chapel and faded murals of Indians, voyageurs and historical characters. The whole place was deserted and decrepit.

"This was built thirty years ago by a Wawa entrepreneur named Al Turcotte," said Donnie. "He visualized it as a tourist attraction, but when Al died the thing just died out."

We drove back to town and Donnie showed me a trapper's cabin built about 1880. It's still standing. Right across the road lives a retired trapper, Clarence Horton, who told us some hair-raising tales such as the time he had to snowshoe fifty miles through the wilderness to get back to Wawa.

Later, we went to a rambling general store on the main street where you can buy almost anything. Sitting outside were farm implements and artifacts from Wawa's mining boom at the turn of the century.

The next day we went fishing on the Magpie River not far from High Falls, which, by the way, is another scenic marvel that brings gasps of admiration from tourists. Donnie caught a 12-pound salmon. I didn't catch any fish, but caught something equally gratifying — a glimpse of a sunrise on Lake Superior's north shore.

Potbellied Pigs

❧

Ordinarily you don't think of potbellied pigs as ideal pets to have around the house. But quite a few people find the little pigs just as lovable as dogs and cats.

I had never seen one until I visited a farm on Cherry Valley Road near Simcoe. The mailbox read: "August Cloet and Girls". August is a beef cattle farmer. The "girls" are his wife, Sue, and their daughters, Kim and Kerry.

When you go past the rambling farmhouse out to the barnyard, you find the Cloet family raises a lot more than beef cattle. Aside from four riding horses, they have an unusual miniature stallion called "C.B.", short for "Cinnamon Britches". In the barn are a couple of rare Barbados sheep named Isaac and Anna. In another part of the barn are African short-haired pygmy goats. But the piece de resistance are the potbellied pigs. There were just three of them when we were there. They're about a foot high and about two feet long. The pigs are registered animals, and those of high quality have a short snout, sparse black coat with white markings, wrinkled jowls and a sagging belly. There is evidence that they've been in existence since 4000 B.C.

They're friendly little critters. Two of them in the barn are named Porkaruse Dynasty and Petunia Dynasty. They're solely for breeding purposes. But the third, Ebony, is a family pet and lives in the house. In many ways the pigs are easier to raise than the usual type of house pets. They don't have fleas, are easily housebroken and absolutely odourless. Ebony loves Flintstone vitamins as snacks.

Sue has been riding horses in competition for 20 years, but lately her main interest has been in rare breeds of animals, and she's especially engrossed in raising the pigs.

"They're wonderful pets," she says, "and are becoming

increasingly popular. They're cuddly, and children love them. Our girls are very attached to them. I've sold a few piglets, but I'm not pushing it. I'm more interested in quality than quantity."

Ebony gets along very well with the two dogs and two cats in the household, but her best friend is a ferret called Gidget. They often sleep together. Then, of course, there are two small hedgehogs to round out the menagerie.

But it's the miniature pigs that are in the spotlight these days. They're pricy, pedigreed little porkers, ranging from $500 to $10,000. And it could be that some day Sue may have a really big thing with her little pigs.

Bagpipe Makers

❧

Bagpipes have always baffled me. Those strange looking contraptions that stick out every which way and emit weird laments, have struck me as something created by a musical misfit in partnership with a deranged craftsman.

I'm fully aware that these are fighting words — out-and-out heresy to a Scot. But bear with me. My ideas have changed radically.

This sudden shift occurred when we spent a day or so hanging around Jack Dunbar's place in St. Catharines. Jack and his partner, Ken Eller, have the distinction of owning what's thought to be the only full-time bagpipe-making plant in North America!

Terry was away at the time, so Global's Rick Dade was our cameraman for the TV item we were doing.

Rick was the one who put us on to the story in the first place. He's a member of the Metro Police Pipe Band and an accomplished piper. Between Jack, Rick, and the four craftsmen at the shop, I picked up enough of the history, the great traditions and the careful crafting of the pipes to make me an overnight aficionado!

"Bagpipes go back to ancient times," said Rick. "In fact, Nero wasn't playing a fiddle while Rome burned, it was an early type of bagpipe."

"Malcolm Canmore was the first king of a united Scotland," piped up Jack. "Around 1068 he organized the first Highland Games, and it was in that period that the basic Celtic bagpipe got its own Scottish identity."

I was impressed still further when one of the craftsmen came over toward us lugging a big chunk of dark wood. "This is African Blackwood," he said. "We make our finest pipes from this. It's the world's heaviest and hardest."

Later I saw some imitation Blackwood being cut to size, bored and drilled. It's commonly used now because it adjusts to climatic conditions.

They showed me how to use a practice "chanter" — the part with the holes. I was able to bring forth a few sounds that I personally found very pleasing to the ear.

As we began shooting the story, my mounting enthusiasm for the pipes knew no bounds. I visualized myself as a lone piper wandering the Scottish glens. Things like that.

Jack told me that until five years ago when the plant opened, most bagpipes used on this continent were ordered from Scotland. But now Canadian pipers need lament no more. They can get supplies right at home.

Jack apprenticed in Scotland, but when he came to Canada in the early fifties, there was no opportunity to work at his craft. He had a variety of jobs and made pipes on the side until he met Pipemaster Ken Eller and they started Dunbar Eller Ltd.

While I was fooling around with my practice chanter, I asked Jack to play something on it.

"I don't play the bagpipes," he said.

I was surprised. "How is that?" I asked.

He looked me at me quizzically for a moment and then said, "Did Stradivari play the violin?"

Rare Breeds

❦

There's a farm in Eastern Ontario that's unique in Canada. Located a few miles from the village of Marmora, Joywind Farm is dedicated to preserving rare or dwindling breeds of livestock.

The farm itself exudes an old world charm. There's a quiet rather quaint atmosphere about it that seems to reflect the old values of plain living and high thinking. There are weathered split rail fences, and fences made of heavy stone. I had a feeling they might have been wrestled from the unyielding land by United Empire Loyalists.

Roaming about the fields and barnyards were types of farm animals I'd never seen before. Or even heard of. There were 4-horned Jacob sheep, an endangered breed. And the rare Barbados Blackbelly, a sheep that grows hair, not wool.

Jy Chiperzak, who started the farm about a decade ago, pointed over to a few cattle standing in the shade of a knarled old apple tree. "There," he said proudly, "is the second largest breeding herd of Irish Kerry cattle in North America."

He went on to say that Kerry cattle arrived in Ireland about 2500 B.C., and County Kerry was named after then, not vice versa. The "herd", as he called it, consisted of a bull, cow and heifer. I began to realize that you have to think in a small way when dealing with rare species.

Chiperzak is something of a rare breed himself. He's a city-bred filmmaker turned farmer, although he still makes an average of two films a year. It was while he was doing a segment on genetics for "The Nature of Things" that he became aware of the necessity of conserving older breeds of livestock.

"We've become so engrossed with productivity and profit," he said, "That we've limited ourselves to fewer and fewer breeds. We're not sure that present breeds will survive environmental changes, and we may eventually have to call upon the genes of ancient types that have managed to come through eons of change."

He took me over to look at what appeared to be a lone pony. "This is the Prezawalski's horse," said Jy. "It's named after the man who rediscovered it and there are only a few hundred remaining. It's the world's only truly wild horse because man never domesticated it. But it's maintained itself over 60 million years of evolution."

Chiperzak is in constant contact with other conservationists of rare livestock scattered throughout the world, and is executive director of Joywood Farm Conservation Inc. which is registered as a non-profit organization.

Jy's wife, Gail, seems just as knowledgeable as he is about the rare livestock. She also helps with the daily chores — as do their children. Their young daughter, Meagan, stayed with us while we toured the farm, and I was thinking that she was fortunate being raised in a setting that would bring many happy memories of her childhood spent amid the quiet beauty of Joywind Farm.

Saga of the Swans

Over the years a lot of interesting things have happened at the Wye Marsh Centre near Midland, what with the bugs, beetles, birds and the millions of little critters that make the marsh their home.

I remember meeting Mac the Falcon, a born actor if I ever saw one. Less ferocious were Bill and Emmy, the world's first radio-equipped turtles who gave biologists a better idea of how turtles go about the business of making a living. Then there was Darth Radar, the huge snapping turtle who could scare the living bejabbers out of you when he was in a bad mood.

But the event that caused the biggest stir was the arrival of a pair of trumpeter swans a few years ago. The swans had been brought from Michigan after lengthy negotiations and considerable expense. What made their appearance so significant was that there had been no trumpeters in Huronia for 200 years!

A section of the marsh was fenced off and the swans were given the V.I.P. treatment. But right off the bat there was a setback. The female died of an infection.

The staff took a deep breath, rolled up their sleeves and began the search for another mate for "Wye", the male swan. It was a tough job, but through networking, another female was found and successfully transported to the marsh. They named her "Marie". There were high hopes that the pair would bond and produce health cygnets, as the offspring are known.

Then one day late in June, Bob Whittan, the Centre's director, phoned me. "Great news," he said excitedly. "Eggs have been laid. This may be it."

At that point the swan area began to resemble an armed camp. It was guarded 24 hours a day and a special watch was put on Darth Radar, the snapper, just in case he got some funny ideas about snatching one of the eggs.

About a month later, two cygnets were hatched and there was joy at the Wye. We went to the marsh the next day. The cygnets were about eight inches long and weighed seven ounces. Terry got some great shots of Wye and Marie swimming beside the little ones. Swans swim as soon as they are hatched, and forage for their own food. But, unfortunately, there was another bitter blow. One of the cygnets disappeared, likely caught by a snapper. It wasn't Darth. He was nowhere near the area at the time.

Even with the one remaining cygnet, it was still a blessed event. After two centuries, the trumpeter swans, once so prominent in the who's who of the Hinterland, had returned to Huronia.

Philosopher's Wool

❦

When Shepherd Eugene Bourgois sheared his sheep and got only 30¢ a lb. for their woolly coats, he had a feeling he was being fleeced. Especially when he knew his wife had paid $22.00 a pount retail for wool to knit a sweater.

One day when he was bleating all the way to the bank, he thought of other shepherds he'd met who were in the same corrall. He set aside his shepherd's crook, got out a pencil and paper and began to figure ways and means of starting what became The Philosoper's Wool Co.

The name was appropriate. Eugene has a Masters Degree in philosophy and was working on a doctorate when he chucked the whole thing and turned to nature and the land.

He'd had a love of nature from childhood, but knew nothing about sheep farming. He managed to scrape together enough money to get 11 acres of scrub land at Inverhuron, up near Kincardine on Lake Huron's shores. He had enough money left over to get 18 sheep.

His flock kept growing. Everything was growing except his income.

But he had figured out a plan, and began to put it into operation. He persuaded about 30 other wool producers around the province to send their wool to him, instead of putting it on the open market.

Eugene sent the raw wool to be processed to his specifications. That included retaining most of the lanolin. The skiens and balls of pure wool that came back were sent to several retailers he lined up. On top of that he engaged a number of knitters who worked mostly in their homes knitting a variety of items like sweaters and scarves. These were also sent to the retailers. As a result, Bourgois and the other producers are now getting a profit of about $2 a pound. And the philosopher gets an extra dollar off the top for his efforts.

These days, Eugene has his own retail outlet as well. It's located in what was formerly a 100-year-old cabin he bought and attached to the back of his house.

When we saw him recently, he had a flock of 69 sheep and 54 spring lambs. The Philospher's Wool Co. was a going concern, and for the philosoper and the other shepherds it's sure made the fleece more golden.

Flag Waver

❦

I like to think of myself as a world citizen. Far above rabid nationalism. Perhaps I am — in theory. I'll discuss "One World" notions and all their ramifications at the drop of a hat. Very lofty stuff. But when it comes to the crunch, I wouldn't want to live anywhere but Canada. And in Ontario at that.

I'm not a flag waver either. When the bit fight was on in 1965 and the first truly Canadian flag was to become the country's symbol over the violent objections of many, I took a detached, somewhat supercilious view of the proceedings as befits any true world citizen. I regarded myself as far above such nonsense. I would look down my nose, rather archly, as I recall, and say, "Does it really matter in the long run?" A very superior approach to the issue.

This didn't bother the Burke family one bit. While I expounded my philosophy at great length, they listened politely but kept on with their work of making flags of all nations at their little shop on the main street in the village of Thornton.

Gordon and Bett Burke had opened "Flags Unlimited" in 1964, just before the big controversy about the Canadian flag. I think all of their eight children were involved in the flag business at one time or another. It seemed to me the small shop was crammed with wall-to-wall Burke children, all scurrying around designing, pinning or sewing flags.

"We haven't had much call for the new Canada flag," said Gordon. "People still want the British Union Jack, or the Ontario flag which incorporates it."

Over the years I went back to see the Burkes every once in a while. The last time was during the 25th anniversary of the Canada flag. The picture had changed radically. "Flags Unlimited" had, of course, grown into the big complex on Highway 400 that's become a familiar sight to motorists going up to cottage country. Gordon had died, but some of the children were still there. Paul Burke and his brother Ed told me that the Canada flag had become their best seller!

I looked around the plant and watched the large staff making colourful flags — some of them flags of nations I've never even heard of. I concluded that my "one world" theory would be a bit difficult to put into practice.

The Burkes gave me a Canada flag as a present. And when I got back to our farm, I hoisted it up on a flagpole out near the garden. It looked impressive. Suddenly, I visualized the wheatfields of the prairies, the foothills of the Rockies, the Maritime fishing villages and the rugged bush country of the north. I decided to do a little flag waving after all.

I went back to "Flags Unlimited" the next day and got an Ontario flag to go with the Canada flag. I guess I'd forgotten there are such things as roots to be considered, even though you're a world citizen.

Hank's Place

Hank Gray has the most unusual apple orchard I've ever seen. It's not a big one as apple orchards go. There are only about 250 trees. But on those trees are close to 175 varieties of applies!

The whole thing started 30-odd years ago when Hank and his wife bought a place at Glenora near the Bay of Quinte.

There were a few scruffy-looking apple trees on the property, and a friend suggested they try grafting a few new varieties on the old trees.

Hank went to one of the many orchards in the area to get an idea of what grafting was all about. While there, he picked up a couple of "scions" — twigs or branches — and in an awkward sort of way grafted them on one of his trees.

To his surprise, one of them clicked! He tried a few more, perfecting his grafting technique of cutting and binding as he went along. He began a study of apples and discovered that some varieties had become almost extinct.

One morning when he was wandering around his five acres of orchard, he got an idea. Why not create an orchard devoted to the preservation of old varieties of apples and possibly develop new ones? It became a retirement project.

"I set a goal of 50 varieties," says Hank. "Then I began travelling around looking for varieties I knew were dying out."

He travelled hundreds of miles in his quest. He talked to big apple growers, or just plain folks who happened to have a few apple trees. He uncovered a strain that originated in old Roman days. He found another of Russian origin. His curiosity became boundless. He forgot his goal of 50 varieties. He just kept on going.

Today, most of the trees are small. All are neatly labelled. They have names like Lady Apris, Maiden Blush and Scarlet Pippin.

"It took me seven years to find a Bell Flower," says Hank, "and longer than that to get a Ben Davis!"

There's a sign outside Hank's place on Glenora Road that reads "Hobby Orchard — Visitors Welcome".

People, including agricultural experts, drop in all the time to take a look at the orchard.

Hank, with his wide-brimmed farmer's hat, round red face and ready smile, likes to saunter with them, give a few tips on grafting and show them his latest discoveries.

Although he's now crowding eighty, he's still the sleuth tracking down elusive varieties of apples, grafting and gathering them together for the preservation of the species.

Gingersnap Junction

❦

We get our birdseed at Gingersnap Junction. If you've ever visited Wasaga Beach, you've likely driven through Gingersnap Junction without ever knowing it.

There are no signs on the highway to indicate you've arrived, and it's not on any map. There are only a few houses, one of them being the farmhouse of Doug and Diane Langman where we get the birdseed.

We've gone through the hamlet many times — on the road from Elmvale to Wasaga — without even knowing its name. We were more interested in the fields of sunflowers growing beside the highway during the late summer months.

Until recent years, fields of sunflowers were a rare sight around the province. Then a few farmers found that sunflower seeds could be a profitable cash crop.

Doug and Diane Langman planted a couple of acres of sunflowers ten years ago, and now have over 100 acres. And they sell about 50 tons of seed a year to bird lovers who know that hungry wintering birds gobble up the seeds with glee.

Doug harvests the crop in October when the blooms have withered and only the round platters of seeds remain. He had to make special attachments for his combine to do the job, and one day we watched him going up and down the many rows, as the seeds spilled into a hopper connected to the combine. The seeds are bagged at a barn near the house, and Diane handles the sales. There are no distribution problems. People drive to the front of the barn and load up for the winter.

When we went to get our usual stock of seeds last fall, we noticed the Langmans had added another room to the farmhouse and had opened a bakery. Diane's cousin, Marie, was doing the baking. There was fresh bread, cakes and sunflower seed cookies. And there was a sign over the entrance reading "Gingersnap Junction Bakery". I asked Doug how the name originated.

"At the turn of the century," he said, "the people living around here used to meet once a week to discuss community affairs. They'd gather at a general store that used to be across the road. The store sold gingersnaps and they'd munch on them during the meeting. So the area became known as Gingersnap Junction, although our mailing address is Elmvale."

You can spot the Langman's place easily. There's a sign on the highway saying "Birdseed for Sale'. That's the only way you'll know you've discovered "Gingersnap Junction".

Uptergrove Railroad

❧

I was too young to ever meet the builders of famous Canadian railways like the CN and CP. They were just slightly ahead of my time. Not much mind you. But far enough that we never had a chance to sit down man-to-man and talk railroads.

Then one day, I met John Smith and Cecil Byers, two young men in their late fifties who are bona fide railroad builders. For eight years, they've been engaged in blending the past and the present into the Uptergrove Shortline Railroad.

John and Cec aren't professional construction men or anything like that. They're a couple of farmers. They're neighbours who still farm the land their grandfathers settled years ago near Uptergrove, a few miles east of Orillia.

"When I was a kid," said John with a faraway look in his eyes, "I'd watch the big CPR trains going through here. So did Cec. We used to count the cars."

When the trains stopped operating after 92 years, John bought the right-of-way, and the pair decided to recreate their memories. That's how the Uptergrove Shortline was born. And it's a railroad with a difference.

Shortline is appropriate. There's just 500 feet of track. Halfway down the track stands the jewel of the line — old No. 46, built in the early 1920s. It's no streamlined silver streak, but it has a style of its own. It has rust. It has bumps. It has bruises. It has the beat-up beauty of age and experience. It's been around.

Surrounding it are four boxcars. Also dilapidated, but intact. Eventually, they'll be able to roll once again, as will old No. 46.

Terry took pictures of John and Cec pushing up and down on their "jigger" — a two man hand car. Then he took a shot of me driving the restored "Velocopede". That's a type of hand car you can use if you want to go it alone. I went skimming along right to the very end of the line, which took about 10 seconds.

One car that's already restored is the caboose. It's in mint condition. Very comfortable. Very posh. Strictly Royal York! It contains photos, artifacts, a little washroom, and details right down to a 1908 payroll book.

John and Cec have great plans. They intend to lay another 600 feet of track, and gather additional equipment. It's quite a project. Where will it all end? When will they complete it? Who knows? At this point, all you can say is "somewhere down the line".

Lady of the Lamp

❧

The village of Elora is one of the most picturesque places in Ontario. With its magnificent Grand River Gorge, tumbling rapids, the restored 19th century shops right out of a Charles Dickens novel and the country luxury of the Elora Mill Inn, the village is a showplace that attracts thousands of tourists annually.

But there's something else which has nothing to do with the spectacular gorge or the beauty of the village, that most people seem to miss.

It's a little church that holds a key which opens your heart to a romantic love story akin to that of Romeo and Juliet.

The church, St. John's Anglican, is just a stone's throw from Mill Street where, especially in the summer, tourists bustle in and out of the shops, boutiques and galleries.

The day I first entered it, some ten years ago, the church was deserted. I walked up to the altar. On the wall to the right of the altar was a faded mural. It showed a woman dressed in what appeared to be a nurse's uniform of yesteryear. Her arms were outstretched and her eyes looked upward.

Directly below, enshrined in a glass case were two silver chalices and a paten used for the bread in communion services. Dated 1952, the Latin on the paten says the set was a gift to "a friend most dear."

It was intriguing and mysterious. Then I picked up one of the small pamphlets placed on a table beside the glass case. It unfolded a fascinating love story.

The woman in the faded mural was Florence Nightingale, the famed "Lady of the Lamp", who achieved world-wide recognition for her pioneering work in nursing during the Crimean War. The "friend most dear" was one of the early ministers of the church, Rev. John Smithhurst.

The pair had met in Derbyshire, England, where Florence Nightingale's father owned estates. Smithhurst was her first cousin. They fell in love, but in Victorian England, marriage between cousins was considered scandalous.

They realized they must separate. But before they said goodbye, they made a pact. He would dedicate himself to missionary work in the Canadian west, while she would learn all she could about nursing as it existed at that time.

John became a highly respected chaplain in the Red River settlement. Florence, although she had received several offers of marriage, continued with her nursing career.

Twelve years later Smithhurst returned to England where the two lovers had arranged to meet again. The subsequent events are vague. It's believed they agreed to remain in their chosen paths.

John was offered a post at the Elora Church. The silver communion chalices were sent by Florence shortly after his arrival. John died in 1867 and is buried in the graveyard beside the church.

When I revisited St. John's recently the mural had been erased — likely too faded to be restored. But is remains in my memory as does the story of the love that was not to be.

But our lives are woven in strange dramatic patterns. If the couple had married and lived happily ever after, the world would never have known "The Lady of the Lamp."

The Goldfields

❧

You get caught up in the romance and adventure of life in Northern Ontario's goldfields. It's not just the history. The spirit of the pioneers still exists. The people are invigorating. They're still a bunch of dreamers.

Seldom is heard a discouraging word. In the restaurants of the hotels where we stay, there's talk of new properties, great assays, as rugged-looking prospectors mingle with engineers and geologists.

But they're conscious of their heritage as well. One day, I wandered over to the Timmins Museum in South Porcupine, where you can see how it all began.

It's a new building located a couple of miles from the old McIntyre Mine. Outside, there's equipment which was used in the old days, including early drills. The first drills didn't shoot out water to keep the dust down. They were known as "widow makers".

Inside is more ancient lore. The first big strikes in the north were around 1909. There are packsacks and picks. Primitive stuff. The bare essentials needed to survive in the scramble for gold.

There are photos of Porcupine in the gold rush days. It was a rough and roaring town — levelled by fire in 1911, but soon built up again. There are shots of prospector Sandy McIntyre and others of his breed who often made and lost fortunes overnight. They worked hard and played hard.

There's a simulated mine stope. A dingy, eerie place. It's supposed to be "Porcupine Pete's" lost gold mine. It turned out the mine never existed at all. It's all part of the myth and legend of the country's biggest goldfield.

You can see the real McCoy — chunks of gold-bearing ore. And the original 1911 Hollinger Stamp, used to stamp the gold bricks produced by the famous mine.

There's mining rescue equipment used underground in the 20s and 30s. And the canary cage. Every mine had a canary. When the canary fell off his perch, it meant there wasn't enough oxygen. Contrary to popular opinion, the canaries didn't die. The miners took their little buddies with them as they hustled out of there.

A modern analogy to the canaries is the herd of buffalo that roam several acres of land beside the huge Kidd-Creek mining complex not far from the museum. They're there to indicate pollution counts. They become ill if there is any excessive pollution. To the best of my knowledge, they've always been hale and hearty.

I drove back to the hotel restaurant to meet Yves St. Jacques, the great guy who for years has been leading us to nooks and crannies of the north.One of our prospector friends Alec Peron was with him. Alec is a third generation prospector. He's big and burly, and epitomizes the spirit of the goldfields. Like the others, he's always full of schemes and dreams. And also, like the others, he has a heart of gold.

The Whittler

❦

The Ontario countryside fairly bristles with interesting and talented people — if you can find them. They're usually tucked away in some village or hamlet, and mostly unknown except by friends and a few neighbours.

I hear about them in strange ways. I write in restaurants or truckstops or wherever I happen to be, and people often stop to tell me about some item they think might make a good yarn.

That's how I heard about George Sheffer. I was sitting in a coffee shop in Midland scribbling away in my scruffy-looking longhand when a lady came over to tell me about a man in the village of Stayner who was an exceptional whittler.

To me, that's news. To most editors and reporters, it would be considered "fluff". Not meaningful "hard" news which includes international news, politics, revolts, murders, fires, crashes and general mayhem.

I thought that way myself during my many years of reporting and editing such tings. But gradually I began to realize that there was joy and humour in life, as well as conflict and misery, and that there were creative people counteracting the destructive forces. I began to search them out.

The whittler in Stayner sounded interesting. Consequently, I "got on the story right away," as they say in the news business. In my case, about three weeks later.

I wasn't disappointed. George Sheffer turned out to be an 80-year-old phenomenon. Using a simple penknife, he had created hundreds of complex treasures on and of wood. There were small replicas of furniture, farm implements, animals, an antique telephone, pliers, scissors and puzzles. There was a chain of 26 pieces of wood he had made when he was just nine years old. The articles hadn't been whittled in sections then glued together. Each one had been carved from a single piece of wood!

On top of all this was Sheffer's collection of different species of wood. He travelled the world to find them, and had acquired 260 varieties from 66 countries!

Along the way he picked up small items of antiquity he'd found appealing. They were in display cases and ranged from African copper to old-fashioned jacks. It added up to a magnificent small museum.

George Sheffer and his museum are not completely unknown and unsung. Busloads of schoolchildren and seniors arrive periodically and he's in demand as a lecturer on woods of the world. I took a last look at the one-room museum and shook my head in wonder.

It's hearing about people like George and his work that make me happy I became a newsman, and came to believe that the little people of the world make the most intriguing stories.

Mennonite Buggies

❦

I suppose you could say the village of Elmira is the buggy capital of Canada.

Located in the Kitchener-Waterloo area, it's the home of many of Ontario's black-garbed Old Order Mennonites who shun the trappings of the 20th Century such as television and automobiles. They stick with the horse and buggy.

That makes Rural Carriage Supplies a busy place, and likely the largest maker of buggies and carriages in the country.

Working in a rambling old barn-like building a few miles out of the village, 12 skilled employees turn out three or four carriages a week, aside from doing repairs and rebuilding.

Some of the carriage makers have been there for years. We watched two of the, obviously Mennonites, who appeared to be in their seventies, putting in the wooden spokes of a wheel.

Nearby, a younger man who looked more like a modern garage mechanic, was hammering a frame together.

There were several completed buggies scattered around. One was the standard black one-seated type which retails at $1,800. Over in a corner was a surrey, and beside it was a vis-a-vis. The kind used by dignitaries for special events.

Lining the stalls were buggies and carriages in crates. They were to be shipped to various parts of the country. And one we looked at was going to Holland.

The whole operation is on one floor. It's dusty, rather dingy and cluttered. But everyone seems to know exactly what they're doing. They move about with quiet confidence.

Even more cluttered is owner Don Buschert's office. There are papers and files and a motley assortment of letters and orders and whatnot. I felt right at home. It reminded me of my den at the farm.

Don is a relative newcomer to the old trade. He's a former high school teacher who decided to take a run at the buggy business.

"I taught for nineteen years and felt like a change," he says. "I've always been interested in mechanical things, especially in transportation. This turned out to be just the thing."

Somewhat surprisingly, Mennonites account for only about 40% of the business. The majority of orders come from people who just like buggies, and are usually quite well-to-do. The carriage trade — literally.

Glassblower

❦

Do you remember the simple joy of blowing bubbles? Reaching into the soapy water with an old clay pipe and creating a wondrous bubble which would float toward the heavens before its brief life span ended suddenly and silently, leaving no trace that it had ever existed at all?

As children, we didn't mind. There was always another bubble to blow in the instinct known as play.

For those who choose wisely the same spirit prevails as we grow older and the same instinct becomes known as work.

Jamie Sherman likely blew bubbles as a child. Now he blows glass in his snug studio in the outskirts of Bracebridge. But there the comparison ends.

His instincts evolved into the intensity, concentration, skill and intuitive feelings of an artist. In this case, the ancient art of glassblowing.

We watched as the tall, lean, bearded artisan pushed the glassblower's rod into a furnace containing a molten brew of alchemist's chemicals needed to make good glass — a fiery mass in a furnace that rivalled Dante's Inferno. The temperature was 2,500 degrees Fahrenheit!

When we pulled out the rod, he rolled around the hot glass it had collected like liquid honey on a spoon. He blew briefly on the rod, and the hot golden fluid expanded slightly.

He worked quickly in the various stages of blowing, swinging to cool it and shaping. He had to. After eight years of glassblowing, he knew what could go wrong. Forty percent of the glass he works with ends up on the recycling bin. It's a tricky process. Perhaps that's one reason why there are only twenty full-time glassblowers in the whole country.

Jamie has an interesting background. He's of the Sherman family, well known in the steel industry. His great grandfather was a foundry worker in New York state. In 1912, two of his sons started what is now Dofasco in Hamilton, and Jamie's father is Chairman of the Board. I asked if any pressure had been put on him to go into the family business.

"Absolutely none", he said, "and I'm grateful for that. I was allowed to follow my own leanings which turned to music at first. Then ten years ago, I began dabbling in glassblowing and it seemed to take over."

He's been extremely successful in the field and has won various awards. The gallery in his studio is filled with shimmering vases and bowls. Their fluid elegance of swirling edges and colour depth is everywhere.

Although the family steel heritage didn't appeal to Sherman, he didn't forsake it completely. As he puts it, he still works in a highly molten medium.

Star Gazing

❦

There are quite a few amateur astronomers around whose gazes are heavenward bent. But there are a few of them who have their own observatories. Especially the kind Syd Dawson has in Kleinberg.

Kleinberg is another of those picturesque villages scattered about the province that has lots of historic buildings, many of them converted into stores, boutiques and antique shops. It also has the famed McMichael Gallery with its magnificent Canadian paintings. Diagonally across the road from the gallery is Syd Dawson's place.

You don't notice it at first because it's set back in from the road amid tall trees that conceal a big rambling old 1850s home called Redcroft. There's a barn nearby, and not too far away on the manicured lawn is the hexagonal-shaped observatory.

The observatory has three stories, is 35 feet high and is the culmination of a dream Dawson had over 40 years ago. Syd built it himself with the help of his wife Eleanor, and their children.

They spent two years planning it, and the dome was finally lifted on by a derrick in 1970. Made of aluminum, it weighs 1,400 pounds.

The ground floor houses the library. That's the Blue Room. the carpet tiles and burlap are all blue. There are shelves of books on astronomy, and files.

You go up the stairs to the Red Room on the next floor. Decorated in red, it's where charts are plotted. On the top floor is the domed observatory.

But the most unusual part of the whole set-up is something the Dawsons added recently — astronomy by computer! A program disc is put into a shiny machine and out comes a printout of what the skies will look like the following night — or any night for that matter.

The three-inch telescope traces what you want to see using the co-ordinates the computer gives it. It's likely the most technologically sophisticated private observatory in the country.

It's not everybody that has an observatory in their backyard. Of course, not everybody could afford it.

Over the years, the cost of putting Syd's dream into operation must have been out of sight. Likely astronomical!

Wheels Within Wheels

❦

Quite a number of people are collectors of antique automobiles, but Bruce McLean of Glencoe is the first person I've met who collects old steering wheels.

Not only that, in his wheel collection are a number of "fatman wheels" as they were called in the automobile's early days. The "fatman" was the forerunner of today's tilting wheel.

Before meeting Bruce, I had thought of the tilting steering wheel as a newfangled item in automotive technology.

But then I saw McLean's collection of about 70 wheels hanging on the walls of his home. Among them were a number of tilting wheels — one dating back to 1905!

"In those days", says Bruce, "car doors were small and seats usually consisted of a non-adjustable bench. The fatman wheel gave the big men, especially those with a paunch, a little extra space."

McLean, who owns 12 antique cars ranging from a 1902 Curved Dash Oldsmobile to a 1965 Mustang, admits his hobby of collecting fatman wheels is "a bit unusual. It just grew out of my fascination with old cars."

He climbed into a Model T Ford to demonstrate. He showed me how the wheel could slide upward or even fold out of his way to the side.

Bruce finds the old wheels at automotive flea markets, mostly in Pennsylvania and Florida. They can cost anywhere from $50 to $400 depending on the condition.

With the help of his wife Fran, he refinishes the wood which makes up the wheel, and polishes the middle hub, made of Bithe's brass or white metal.

He says he admires the craftsmanship that went into the construction of the wheels.

"Some of them are remarkable" he said pointing to the walnut steering wheel from a 1920 Pierce-Arrow luxury car. "The woodwork is exceptional. You couldn't even make these today."

Finger-grooves in the steering wheels had to be individually sanded out of the wood instead of being cut.

Bruce would like to expand his wheel collection. But it will be a slow process. He can't trade with others. To the best of his knowledge he's the only person collecting such an item.

Meanwhile, the supply of fatman wheels is getting thinner and thinner.

Flower Power

❧

People who move with the flow of nature have learned one of the great secrets of life. They don't fight or mutilate their surroundings. They cherish and protect them.

You sense this deeply-rooted consciousness up at the tip of the Bruce Peninsula. Those who live around the Tobermory area are quietly proud of the gifts nature has given them. And especially of their wild orchids.

The district is one of the best on the continent to see a variety of the magnificent plants that have been growing there since the last ice age.

Every year from May to October, hundreds of naturalists called "orchid hounds" travel from faraway places to see the orchids. Armed with their binoculars and cameras, they roam the trails for miles looking for some of the 48 species that may be peeking out from escarpment cliffs or nearby limestone bedrock shores.

We visited the Bruce when the yellow lady slippers were in bloom. Naturalist Mark Wiercinski was our guide. He's a lean, bearded young man who's been at one with nature since childhood.

He took us to Dorcus Bay near Tobermory. The yellow lady slippers were scattered in patches. There were thousands of them.

Others, such as the ramshead, were harder to find. We were able to locate a couple, but also saw various different kinds of wildflowers like carnivorous insect-trapping pitcher plants.

Along the way, Mark was telling us that the Bruce is blessed with so many species of orchids because of the varied habitats in the area.

We went back to Tobermory and took a boat over to Flower Pot Island. There was a northwest wind blowing and Georgian Bay was rough. After we docked, we walked a nature trail for about a mile, and finally located what Mark had been looking for — a calypso orchid. "It's one of my favourites," he said, "rare in this country, and even in North America."

I've always thought of orchids as delicate flowers that have to be cultivated with care. Mark pointed out that only tropical orchids need pampering.

Those that grow at the Bruce are hardy plants. The only pampering they get is the adulation of admirers, intrigued by the wild orchids' sheer flower power.

Damn Nuisance

❧

Huronia is a hotbed of history. And, indirectly, I've seen it unfold. I've watched it being recreated around the Southern Georgian Bay area that encompasses Huronia.

Years ago, I remember archaeologists sifting through the rubble at what is now the reconstructed Ste. Marie Among the Hurons, near Midland.

As a bushy-tailed newsman, I'd shuffle along beside crusty Dr. Wilf Jury and his knowledgeable wife Elsie, as Ste. Marie, Ontario's first community to be inhabited by Europeans, gradually came to life again.

I remember Dr. Jury once called me a "damn nuisance" because I asked so many questions. I also remember one of the first stories I wrote while in the area was about Wilf Jury himself.

That "doctor" moniker was an honourary degree given to him by The University of Western Ontario. So they could make him head of the archaeology department I guess.

He only got as far as Grade Six in school. When I saw Elsie a few years ago she said, "He lied to you. It was only Grade Five."

He didn't have much schooling, but he had an excellent education. And there's a big difference.

Over the years he amassed an amazing collection of Indian artifacts and became a world authority on Indian archaeology. Ste. Marie was just one of his projects, but likely the best known.

Since it was completed, over a million visitors have been taken back in time to 1649. That's when the Jesuits and lay people from France along with their Huron allies, set up the community on the shores of the Wye River, the highway to Georgian Bay.

Today you can see costumed Jesuits, craftsmen at work, native people cooking over fires, gardeners, all busily engaged in the drama of carving a niche in the wilderness that became Ontario.

Events are reenacted. More French settlers arrive bringing news from home. They come up the Wye River in canoes and carry supplies from Quebec.

There's a great whoop-de-do. There's shouting and laughter. Old friends meet again. Sometimes you feel like an intruder.

The original Ste. Marie didn't last very long. Ten years after it was built, the settlers and Hurons burned it before the advancing Iroquois attacked. They fled to Christian Island a few miles away.

That's where I met Elsie Jury again for the first time in a long while. Now in advanced years, she was watching a "dig" as archaeologists, some she had taught, were probing for the village where the settlers had built another new community.

She's still active. She has an office in an archaeological museum in London dedicated to her husband. She goes in a few days a week "to take care of Wilf's stuff".

Bad Luck Gull

❦

There's a seagull named Clifford who hangs out at a marina on Southern Georgian Bay. He's very popular, and has become quite a celebrity. For good reason. He's a peg-legged gull!

Clifford no longer flies through the air with the greatest of ease. He just clip-clops around the repair shop at Butler Marine in Penetanguishene, oblivious to smiling spectators.

While other seagulls are looked upon with mixed emotions by most people, Clifford inspires interest and admiration in all.

When he feels like taking a rest, he has a cardboard box with his name on it where he can hole up for awhile. He doesn't have to scrounge around for food like others of his kind. People are always giving him titbits.

He appears to be quite satisfied with his lifestyle, which

strangely enough, started with a run of bad luck.

It all began about a year ago when Clifford was hit by a car and one of his wings was broken. He was found by Dan Fraser, manager at the marina, who gave the young gull a warm and safe home for the winter.

"He could never fly again," says Fraser. "He'd walk around the shop waiting for the coffee truck to come along, and people gave him scraps from their lunches. Under the circumstances, he led a good life."

But Clifford was one of the roving kind. One day he wandered out of the workshop and on to a busy street. He was hit by a car again. When Fraser located him, his other wing was broken and his leg mangled.

"I took him to a vet, but they couldn't do much for him," said Dan. "It was hard for him to hop, so I made him a wooden leg. He caught on to it pretty fast and started to clip-clop along."

Clifford did so well with his new leg that he went on another journey. He roamed about two miles to the downtown area to visit the Dock Lunch, one of his old haunts.

It's amazing that he didn't get clobbered again, but when Fraser went down to get him, he seemed to be all right. He brought him back to the shop and Clifford slept in his box for the rest of the day.

"He just seems to have bad luck," Dan mused as he held Clifford in his arms. "One time he swallowed a sparerib bone that got stuck in his throat. I had to take him to the vet again."

Although he can no longer swoop and soar like his buddies, Clifford's new life has its compensations. He has a comfortable year-round home, lots of friends and plenty of food.

Paradoxically, his bad luck has brought him good fortune. For all we know, he may be thinking, "By Gully, I never had it better!"

Old Mill

❦

At the turn of the century, every Ontario town or village worth its salt had its own mill. Now there are just a handful left.

The Backus Mill near Port Rowan has been restored, and operates for visitors in the summer months as an historical attraction. And there are a couple of others like it, with water wheels and everything, in heritage villages.

But there's an old flour mill in the Georgian Bay village of Coldwater that's still going full blast commercially. It hasn't stopped since it was built in the 1830s, and the new owner is kept hopping, taking care of business.

Arend Meiling bought the mill a few years ago. He'd been a restaurateur for 17 years, both here and in his native Holland, and knew absolutely nothing about mills. I was curious about his abrupt switch.

"I felt like a change," he said in his Dutch accent, "and I liked the mill as soon as I saw it. I liked the gable roof, and the windows and the board and batten siding. I especially liked the smell of it. It has a clean, country smell."

Historians find the old mill's background intriguing. Originally, it was called "The Indian Mill" because several bands of Indians, as well as British immigrants, first settled in the area, which is not too far from Orillia. The Indians called the budding community Coldwater, because of the fast-flowing river that ran through it. The mill was built beside the river and was one of the earlier structures in the village.

Arend runs the mill by himself. The ancient hopper, crusher and mixer turn farmers' grains into barley, wheat and oats. He often bags 12 tons of corn alone in a two or three week period. His customers come from a hundred mile radius. Some families have been using the mill for generations.

Arend loves the old mill as well as his new career as a miller. But obviously, there are times when a business like that can become a real grind.

Custom Canes

❦

There's a business that operates out of a home on Main Street in Cambridge called "Cane and Able".

You can not only choose from what may be the best selection of hardwood canes in Canada, but also get a concise course in the history and manufacture of them as well, from Jill Summerhayes who started the business a few years ago.

After you've talked to Jill for awhile, you take a new look at canes. She's an authority on the subject. She travels coast to coast giving lectures and seminars about canes and walking sticks.

She'll order any kind of cane you want from any part of the world and adjust it to your height on machines in her basement workshop.

She doesn't expect to make a fortune in the enterprise. But she's done well enough to open two outlets in the west and one on the east coast.

Oddly enough, the business was born of adversity. Two years ago, Jill contracted osteoarthritis and needed a cane to get around. The vivacious 45-year-old reacted negatively to the idea. She felt that her active, busy lifestyle had come to the end.

She found herself trying to hide the cane from people. Then she realized she was taking a stereotypical view of walking sticks. She decided to try to regard the cane as a fashion accessory.

"I started by tying silk scarves on the cane to match my outfits," she says. "Then one night when my husband and I were going to a party, I wore flowers around the cane, and everybody complimented me. So I made a few corsages for it."

She became interested in the history and manufacturing of canes. While researching, she found that from biblical times canes have reflected changing cultures and civilizations.

"Henry VIII owned magnificently jewelled canes," Jill explained. "And during the 18th century, canes became an essential part of the wardrobe. Both men and women often had more canes than pairs of shoes."

Times changed and canes were no longer fashionable. Summerhayes discovered that these days about the only canes you could buy were those plain utilitarian ones you get in drug stores or hospitals.

She decided to start a business selling canes that had a bit of flair. Since there were few Canadian suppliers, she began to import more from other parts of the world. Today she has more kinds of canes than you can shake a stick at.

There's an elegant ebony stick with a silver handle, one that's glass blown from a whisky bottle, one like those used by the Six Nations Band for special occasions — a magnificent selection.

So in just four short years, Jill has turned the tables. Instead of a cane, she has a good business to lean on, while also returning the walking stick to a fashionable symbol — raising canes to new heights.

Dupper Don

❦

You can watch the squat little boats chug past the historic lighthouse on the pier, you see the fisherfolk moving around on this, readying the catches they'll drop off at one of the processing plants on the harbour's shoreline.

Port Dover is about the closest thing you'll find in the province to fishing villages in the Maritimes. Some of the weatherbeaten fishermen have been challenging the treacherous Lake for generations.

One of them is "Dupper Don" Mummery, who began fishing when he was 14, and spent the next 45 years bringing in catches in all sorts of weather — from the calm waters rippling in the summer sunrise, to the mad March days when the tugs are tossed and tumbled as they struggle out to the nets.

I'd seen Dupper (nobody knows how he got the nickname) many times in the Knechtel's Dairy Bar where I go to scribble stories when working around Dover. For years, he's been one of the coffee regulars which include other fishermen (and women), along with assorted artists, artisans, merchants, naturalists, the odd politician and — for good measure — a burly policeman.

But I'd never really talked to the quiet, husky fisherman until I heard he had retired; he had left the lake to make the ship's wheels. One big wheel looked like the work of a master craftsman. I was curious, and asked him how long he'd been working with wood.

Dupper chuckled. "About 30 years, I guess," he said. "While I was fishing for a living, I made nine fishing boats in my spare time."

I suppose that's common knowledge around Dover, but it was surprising news to me. I asked a few more questions and learned that his grandfather had come to Dover from England where he'd been a fisherman, as had his father before him. When Dupper began carrying on the tradition, he worked for a while for various fishermen, then decided to build his own boat, although he knew absolutely nothing about boatbuilding.

"I didn't have any plans," he said. "I just got some scrap and did the best I could. Everybody around here said I was crazy, but it turned out all right. I got interested and made the eight other boats when I wasn't fishing."

As I sauntered off, I began to think of how little we know about people we meet casually. In Dupper's case, he struck me as an easy-going guy who wouldn't do any more than he had to. But in his "retirement", shearing and chipping away at wood, he's as busy as ever.

And between the fish and chips, he's sure living a full life.

Fiddler's Cove

❦

There are enough violins and violas at "Fiddler's Cove" to supply a symphony orchestra. There are also ancient pianos, harpsichords, mandolins and a variety of other stringed instruments.

"Fiddler's Cove" is what collector George Smith calls the big basement room in his Simcoe home, where his unusual assortment of instruments is displayed.

Along with the violins and so on, are seven vintage pianos including a rare Weber piano made in 1875, which George has restored, and an old rebuilt organ from 1900. The two genuine dulcimers he has are likely the most exotic in the collection. The dulcimer is an instrument that originated in Russia long before the first piano-type instruments were made.

But George is more than just a collector. He's an artisan and craftsman who has made eight of the violins displayed, and a couple of magnificent mandolins, along with a huge harpsichord that looks very much like a grand piano.

We watched him as he was making a viola in his workshop, using tools he made himself. He was 74 at the time, and I'd assumed the work was a retirement project. But it turned out he'd been building one thing or another since childhood.

"When I was a child, my family didn't have much money," he said, "and we'd use my father's tools to make our own toys. I've been building ever since — including this house."

I asked him how he had learned to make the complex instruments. "From books," he said. "Libraries are wonderful assets to any community."

Another unusual thing about George is that what he makes, he plays. He has learned to play almost every instrument he has, and is in demand at everything from fiddling groups to entertaining at nursing homes.

As he played the violin, I accompanied him on one of the ancient pianos to the tune of "Whispering", a song from the early thirties. The piano was older than our combined ages, which made it a real antique.

The Misfit Hill

❦

I worked in Timmins as a newsman in the late 40s and still get up there frequently to do television stories. I thought I knew the major points of interest pretty well, but late one February, I came upon something that had escaped me completely.

It's a hill in Timmins that's the only one of its kind on the continent. Not only that, the ski resort built below it is operated by a family of world class skiers.

The hill is called Mount Jamieson. It has a 350 foot vertical drop. That isn't high as ski hills go. But it's cone-shaped, like a volcano. It stands out like a sore thumb because the land for miles around is relatively flat.

It seems that during the glacial age, Mother Nature pulled a fast one and Mt. Jamieson became a geological mistake. The only other hill like it is in South Africa and, coincidentally, is located in goldfields, as is Timmins.

The Timmins Ski Club moved to Mt. Jamieson in 1945 and in more recent years the Kreiner family of Timmins, and a group of investors, developed it into what's now known as the Kamiskotia Ski Resort.

If you're at all interested in skiing, you'll remember the Kreiner sisters who were Olympic champions in the 70s. Karen Kreiner was the only Canadian gold medallist in the 1976 winter Olympics. Her younger sister Laurie, an Olympic finalist, was, at

14, the youngest skier to ever win a national championship. That record still stands. Their father, Dr. H. O. Kreiner, was the National Ski Team's first doctor.

Laurie now runs the resort. She knows a lot about the hill. She described it as a "geological misfit" and gave me the complex details of its formation.

The Kreiner sisters both learned to ski at Mt. Jamieson, and when we were there, about 50 children were out on the slopes with their ski instructors.

It may not be the Rockies or the Alps, but the old hill has a style of its own and may become the home of still more great champions.

Feast of Fantasy

❦

I met Macbeth, Henry VIII, The Three Musketeers and a host of other characters from the pages of classical literature at a little red schoolhouse near the village of Brunner, north of Stratford.

Macbeth wasn't scrapping with Macduff, the Musketeers weren't engaged in swordplay and Henry VIII wasn't gorging himself. They were just standing around minding their own business. None of them moved a muscle. Of course, they were all made of papier mache.

The creators of these magical figures are Jan and Jean Bajer who live in the schoolhouse, which they've converted into a studio and home. Jean became interested in papier mache while at the Ontario College of Art, and has been turning out the beautifully crafted figures, ranging in size from six inches to three feet or more, for over three decades. Jan's primary talent is creating porcelain pieces which he studied in his native Austria. Aside from making utility items, some of his work is sheer fantasy. There are castles, fire-eating dragons and other figures relating to medieval lore.

For a while the couple stayed with their individual specialties. Then they became interested in each other's work. As Jean says, "we started to teach each other." Now they work together in both porcelain and papier mache.

When we were there, Jan was making a figure of Don Quixote — he of the impossible dreams. Jean had almost completed a colourful model of Katisha, the nasty old lady in *The Mikado*.

Both artists are interested in theatre and that is reflected in much of their work. They begin by drawing sketches of their subjects. Then they build armatures of wood, chicken wire and coat hangers. After that, a rough cover of paper is put on. The paper could be anything from paper towels to newspapers. The design is crafted and held together with wallpaper paste, and finally the piece is painted, usually in vivid hues. None of their work is sent to retailers. It's sold at shows and galleries.

They keep many of their favourite pieces for themselves. And as you wander around the studio and other rooms of their home, your imagination gets free rein as you gaze at the myriad of wondrous creations. From ferocious-looking dragons to Little Bo Peep, it's all a feast of fantasy.

Paula's Products

❦

On the main street of the quiet village of Blackstock, north of Oshawa, there's a one-room turn-of-the-century schoolhouse.

It blends in with the few shops and houses along the picturesque tree-lined street, and ordinarily you wouldn't particularly notice it at all.

But inside the little building things are humming. It's a hive of activity. Paula Lishman and 17 other women are bustling around, operating a million dollar business that's known in fashion centres the world over. They're sewing and knitting fur!

Around the village, 60 other women are doing the same thing in their own homes.

In the basement of the schoolhouse, hides of beaver, coyote, mink and fox are laid out on tables. In the background, hanging on racks, are jackets and coats of fur — but fur on the inside as well as outside! Unique fur garments! The process is patented.

The whole thing started just a decade ago when Paula, a housewife and mother of three, was contemplating ways of making a few extra dollars.

Brought up in Labrador, she was taught how to sew, knit and work with leather by her Swedish mother.

When her father, a government meteorologist, was transferred to Toronto, she was surprised to see people wearing fur coats with the fur on the outside.

"In Goose Bay," she said, while showing us around, "lots of people wore fur, but never on the outside. They'd wear muskrat or raccoon fur inside their coats for warmth."

It gave her an idea. She cut scraps from old fur she picked up, sliced them into narrow strips and started to knit them while sitting in front of the fireplace.

Then she developed a system for making strips of fur into durable fur yarn, which she worked in with cotton or silk fibres. Then she weaved fur into the knitting.

She made a few articles and took them to a fur fair. Buyers snapped them up and ordered more.

She knew she had a unique product. She got a loan and taught local women how to knit fur. The business boomed!

Today, Paula Lishman is constantly on the go — family, business, travel to fashion centres in Europe and Asia.

In just a decade, she has parleyed her idea into something that has added another dimension to the fur industry.

Schemes and Dreams

❦

Earl Putnam was 93 when I met him. Nothing too unusual about that. I've met quite a few 93-year-old men. But none quite like Earl Putnam.

He's a builder. A developer of condominiums — for seniors! He was finishing off a development for them called "King Solomon's Place" in Port Elgin, north of Kincardine in Western Ontario.

I spent a day with him. He showed me around the cosy condos of King Solomon's Place. He told me about his newest project in nearby Southhampton. It was to be a 20 million dollar set up. For seniors of course, with Cape Cod style houses.

I had a hard time catching up with Earl. He had been in Florida when I first called. He wasn't down there on a holiday. He was there in connection with a high rise he built for seniors in Sarasota. When we did meet, I had difficulty adjusting to the idea that he was in his nineties. He appeared to be a man in his mid-fifties. He talked fast, walked fast, moved fast. He was lean, light, erect and dapper. He had a booming voice that reverberated around the coffee shop where we had arranged to meet.

He was telling me about the King Solomon development before we went to see it. He gesticulated to emphasize his points. He waved his arms about to include everyone in the coffee shop. And everyone was listening. They had no choice. They were local people and they knew Earl Putnam — a born salesman!

"The seniors snapped up the first 21 units in 23 days," he boomed. "Who wouldn't at $36,000 and $12,000 for the land? It was a steal!"

"Those old people are the salt of the earth," he added, waving an arm over toward King Solomon's Place, just next door to the coffee shop. "They've worked hard, they deserve the best but they don't get it!" He pounded the table and just about spilled our coffee.

Like so many other entrepreneurs I've known, Putnam was a Grade 9 dropout. A farm boy, he ended up in the insurance business, eventually as owner of Canada Health and Accident. He sold it 1967 and retired for two days. Just two days! That was it!

"I look upon retirement as merely a status symbol," he shouted to the audience. "It's really the first step in suicide when you lose your schemes and dreams."

When I asked him the secret of his vibrant health and vitality, he answered simply, "stay active and eat sensibly, but most of all have dreams."

Later we went over to the new development in Southampton. There were 44 acres of beautiful land with a stream running through it. A barn had been converted into a community centre.

I was thinking that "the old people" as Earl called them, would really enjoy it.

Magnificent Obsession

❦

Visualize enough massed brass bands to fill Maple Leaf Gardens and more. There would be over a thousand trumpets, bugles, trombones and other brass instruments.

Visualize all of them hanging in the basement of a country home. Then add to that a motley assortment of ancient horns and bugles with mind boggling names.

That's what you see in the basement of Henry Meredith's home near the village of Arva, north of London.

The immediate impact as you go down the stairs and into the basement is one of surprise and amazement! Terry's Irish eyes twinkled. You could see that he anticipated a great shooting session with the camera.

Jenny's reaction was a bit different. "How would you ever keep them clean?" she wondered.

Meredith's wife, Victoria, glanced over to her. "Don't look at me," she said. "He does it himself."

The collector, Dr. Meredith or 'Hank' as he's generally called, teaches and lectures in music at the University of Western Ontario.

He began the collection casually enough 14 years ago, picking up a few unusual brass or reed instruments at antique shows and flea markets.

Then he got the bug. He started to go further afield looking for instruments. The Meredith home began to bulge. The basement was set aside for the instruments, some badly in need of repair. He'd get them restored.

The collection grew and grew. Now he has what's thought to be the biggest collection of its kind on the continent!

His enthusiasm is contagious. He blew a few notes on what looked a bit like an alto sax, but with a trumpet mouthpiece. Speaking rapidly, he gave me a brief history of it.

"It's a great one," he said, gazing at the strange creation with admiration. "It's called an ophicleide, which translated means 'keyed serpent' and gave Adolph Sax the idea of inventing the saxophone."

We saw horns used in Tibetan temples, horns from Israel and Syria. You name it. Hank likely has it.

But Dr. Meredith also makes use of the old instruments. He's organized a number of early music ensembles which enables him to perform early music on authentic trumpets.

He admits that his interest in the collection has become something of an obsession. But for a man whose whole life revolves around music, it's a magnificent obsession.

Rowing Shells

❦

When I was a youngster I used to hang around rowing clubs a lot. My older brother was an oarsman and I'd often tag along when he was training or racing in the Canadian Henley, Hanlan's Point, or sometimes in the States.

But until recently, I had no idea how racing shells were made — those sleek, slim crafts I'd seen so many times cutting through the water rowed by crews of eight, four, pairs of single scullers.

The Old Master among Canadian buildings of racing shells is located in the village of Lucan — of all places!

That's the village considered the country's most lawless town back in the days of the notorious Donnelly family and the vigilantes who brutally murdered them. Today, Lucan is a peaceful Western Ontario village north of London and off on a side street is the rambling building with a small sign that reads Kaschper Racing Shells.

Inside the plant, 23 skilled craftsmen turn out 15 to 20 shells a month that are shipped to various rowing clubs around the world. The founder of the firm is 53-year-old Jacob Kaschper who apprenticed as a shell builder at the age of 15 in his native West Germany. He's an amiable, knowledgeable boat builder who makes the shells from scratch.

They're made of ash, mahogany and sitka spruce. There are moulds for the 57-foot, eight crew shells down to the 27-foot singles. The outfitting for them is all done right at the factory. Jacob showed us pictures of Kaschper shells being raced at the famed Henley in England, and in Moscow.

"But things are changing," Jacob told us. "The trend today is to synthetic shells. We researched for several years before we started to build them. It meant new designs and a new approach."

The synthetics, made of fibreglass and graphite, are rapidly taking over at the Kaschper plant, although wood is still preferred by the traditionalists, which include the Canadian teams.

Kaschper's son Jurgen is a specialist in making oars. His synthetic prototypes are already in use, and apparently are the only ones on the market made in a single piece.

By the way, with a volume of about 200 shells a year being manufactured, the Kaschper factory is thought to be the largest of its kind on the continent!

It's another of those nooks and crannies around the province you find in unexpected places. In this case, the little village of Lucan.

Crafty Eggs

❦

Have you ever heard of "pysanky"? Not likely, unless you're Ukrainian or have an interest in it. It's the art of painting eggs.

You've likely seen the eggs at one time or another. They're multi-coloured with complex designs. Ukrainian people give them as gifts, or exchange them with friends and use them as decorations all year round. What's left over, they sell at craft shows or church bazaars.

It's an ancient art that's been passed down from generation to generation. And recently, we saw four generations of one family painting eggs at a parish hall in the village of Waterford, south of Brantford.

Pauline Procyk, the great-grandmother of the family, taught her daughter Nancy Sywak, who taught her daughter Anne, who in turn taught her two young sons, Stephen and Darryl.

We got them all together and Terry took pictures of them as they began painting the eggs with that time-honoured craftsmanship that's so lengthy and intricate.

Some of the eggs were wooden, imported from the Ukraine. Others were of Styrofoam, sent from Poland. But most were turkey, duck and chicken eggs from local farms.

The designs were put on with a stylus, then coloured, and allowed to dry. Then additional designs were put on. We didn't see them complete anything because it takes up to 14 hours to craft just one egg!

However, Anne had brought along about one hundred or more finished eggs that were magnificent examples of beauty and artistry. She told us that each colour and design has meaning. For example, yellow represents wisdom, circles portray eternity, animals stand for prosperity and birds for rebirth.

Anne was saying that although traditionally the art has been done by women, in more recent years men have become interested in it. "Thinking back," said Anne, "I remember my uncle was quite accomplished in designing, and I learned as much from him as I did from my mother."

It's not everyone who can acquire sufficient expertise to turn out such beautiful works of art. It takes knowledge, skill and plenty of patience.

Jenny, who was watching one of the women using a stylus with meticulous care, shook her head and said, "You'd need the hands of a surgeon and the patience of Job."

Singing Priest

❦

I met Father Mark Curtis at a recording studio. Although he's a parish priest at St. Joseph's Catholic Church in Guelph, he has another career — he's a composer and recording artist known as "The Singing Priest".

He's a big, round-faced, friendly, personable man who smiles a lot. On the surface, easy-going and full of fun.

He was at the studio to make another record. I sat in the control room with Barbara Myers of Evergreen Records.

Through a wide window, we could see Father Mark at a microphone in the adjacent sound-proof room. He began to sing one of the many songs he has written, a back-up band in the shadows.

I'm not a great fan of today's pop music. I grew up in the era of George Gershwin and Cole Porter and regard most of the current stuff with feelings ranging from amused indulgence to downright contempt.

Bur Father Mark's mellow tenor voice and the soft-rock rhythms of the band lulled me into enchantment and thoughtfulness as I listened to lyrics about life and love, joys and sorrows.

I was thinking both the words and music he writes must spring from his background of experience in his work of helping people, and as a result, his two careers have become intertwined.

Later, as we talked, he told me that was exactly what had happened. He was expressing in his music what he had learned in helping others with their lives.

I asked him how he found time to handle both careers. "Sometimes it's tricky," he laughed. "There are days when I say three masses, have two baptisms, hear five confessions and make a couple of visitations before getting to a concert that night."

At the time I met him, he had completed four records and had just returned from a six-week concert tour. Wherever he goes, he packs the house and has fans of all ages and all walks of life.

After expenses, anything he makes from records or concerts goes to charity. Bookings and other details are handled by his producer and his publicist.

Father Mark is obviously taking it all in stride. He's a relaxed, happy man who has two careers that mesh — one at the altar, and one as his altar-ego — "The Singing Priest".

Jang's Mushrooms

❦

Si Chang Jang has a big woodlot on his 100-acre farm near Green's Corners. Five-foot logs of oak are stacked teepee fashion in clearings and mushrooms are growing out of the logs!

They're big brown mushrooms called shiitake — the type that's grown in Jang's native Korea. And Jang says it's the first mushroom farm of its kind in Canada.

Si Chang is no novice in growing the crop. His family have been mushroom farmers for three generations and he says Southern Ontario is ideal for such farming.

He's a rather short, stocky man in his forties, an entrepreneur who already has a couple of farms — one in Korea and one in Japan.

He bought the former tobacco farm just west of Simcoe three years ago."I wanted to try something new," he said in halting English. "The kind of mushrooms we grow are just starting to become popular in North America. What we need is plenty of wood. As we use it we plant more trees."

He showed me the growing process right from the creation of spores developed in his small sterile lab to the boring of logs and the impregnating of them with the spawn, then sealing the holes with paraffin.

In cold weather the logs are moved into a large plastic-covered greenhouse and the shiitake mushrooms appear in about six months. They're picked by hand and shipped either fresh or dried.

Jang also grows oyster mushrooms. For these he uses poplar. The spawn is put on the ends of the logs and the logs are sandwiched together. The spawn seeps down into them and the light-coloured oyster type later appear out of the sides of the logs.

I've seen a few mushroom farms around the province where

the mushrooms are grown in manure and in the dark. I'd never heard of Si Chang's methods.

The closest approach to the way we farm them is the second way of growing the oyster product. He has a shed where in a dim, warm environment the spawn is put into wheat straw, not manure. The big white oyster mushroom flourishes in it.

Asians look upon the shiitake variety as extremely nutritious food and it's been a staple in their diet for centuries. Currently, Jang's big market is in the U.S., but it's available in some Canadian health food stores.

By the way, Jang uses only the tops of the trees so the oak plantation is a sort of "reforestation" project, rejuvenating the soil and animal habitat.

His gamble seems to be paying off. His storage section is packed with cases for shipment. And apparently the venture is a success mainly because of the oak.

Dollhouse Maker

❧

Some people begin a hobby in childhood and pursue it throughout their lifetime. Others, like Oshawa's Woody Band, latch on to something in their retirement years, and it becomes an absorbing interest almost overnight.

Woody, a former General Motors executive, started to make dollhouses as a distraction. About six years ago, while he was waiting for surgery after a heart attack, his wife and children bought him a dollhouse kit. They were likely thinking of his father, Percy Band, a well-known Canadian collector who had built a big dollhouse. (Today, it's part of a toy exhibit along with the Percy Band collection of antique toys at Black Creek Pioneer Village in Toronto.) But, for Percy Band, building the dollhouse was a one-shot pastime! For his son, making that first dollhouse was the beginning of a complete change of lifestyle.

Since then, Woody Band has completed several dollhouses. And they're magnificent! All of them are furnished, wallpapered and wired. There are also seven box rooms, including a Victorian front hall, an antique shop, a reception hall and a tea room with real-looking cakes and pies. He's recently completed a 1920s butcher shop, and when we saw him, he was planning to build a Southern plantation house.

Not too long ago, he won first prize at Ontario's only juried dollhouse show for his bake shop and tea room. And all this after only six years of working at the craft!

Woody was telling me that dollhouses were made as far back at 1557, but they were always replicas of houses, belonging to royalty, and commissioned as art objects rather than toys.

Dollhouses as we know them today became playthings for children in the late 19th century. They were educational toys used to train young girls of wealthy families to run their future homes.

Today, building or collecting them has become an intriguing hobby. Woody says his greatest satisfaction comes from the reactions of children who see his exhibits at shows and galleries.

But I have a feeling he also gets a creative surge of fulfilment when he first turns on the switch and lights up his "small wonders".

The Healing Brew

❦

I've quaffed the odd cup of herbal tea from time to time and found it a refreshing change. Besides, it's given me a fleeting feeling of self-righteousness that I've risen above my usual caffeine-oriented ways.

But I never became really interested in herbs until I met Jan Longboat. She's a wise woman in her middle years who has the quiet serenity you sense so frequently in native people.

As a child, she learned much about herbs and healing at her grandmother's knee. But later, she also studied for four years at the School of Natural Healing in London, Ontario to become a qualified natural health practitioner. These days, aside from having a private practice, she teaches at Mohawk College.

Her "clinic" is in her beautiful woodsy home near Little Buffalo, south of Brantford. The medicines she dispenses come from her garden of herbs as well as those she gathers in the spring and the fall from the forests and the fields. Jan uses herbs with both familiar and unfamiliar names like sage, hyssop, coltsfoot and April King. The herbs are dried for lengthy periods, then ground in a mill and kept in jars in a small room off the kitchen of her home.

Jan treats people for everything from arthritis to the common cold. Camomile is used for sleeping, comfrey for healing a rash or bee sting. A drink containing burdock is for internal cleansing. It must be started on the day of the new moon and carried through a 28-day cycle.

If such things strike you as mere superstitions in this materialistic age, it should be remembered that many centuries-old, tried-and-true healing techniques have been lost in the scientific shuffle. And many are being revived with some success.

But Jan believes that true healing must being from within. "It begins with the mind, both physically and spiritually," she says. "The negativity of stress, anger and guilt must be erased for holistic medicine to be effective."

By the way, just in the realm of trivia, I discovered that the word "herbs" can be pronounced with the "h" being sounded, or with the "h" being dropped as in "erbs". Apparently, it's optional.

Characteristically, Jan says, "whichever way you find most comfortable."

Having a Wonderful Time

ॐ

Since the turn of the century, postcards have let the pictures do the talking, for those who travel the world, or just for friends and relations on weekend vacations who forward the familiar "Having a wonderful time — wish you were here." But to postcard collectors like Harry Schoon of Oshawa, they're intriguing slices of history.

Harry works at General Motors and when he's not assembling automobiles, he's assembling postcards. His "specialty" takes in an area from Pickering over to Cobourg. He has albums upon albums of cards from that district. You could spend hours leafing through the pages gazing at the postcards of yesteryear he has so carefully inserted.

Around General Motors, Harry is known as "Mr. History". He has picture postcards of G.M. dating back to Sam McLaughlin's Carriage Company, and the early automobiles before McLaughlin teamed with Buick. Along with that are old calendars, photos of conventions and other collectors' items from 60 to 90 years ago.

He has a picture of Whitby's main street that brought back memories. One of my first jobs as a newspaper reporter was at the Whitby paper well over half a century ago. And Harry has a shot of the courtroom where I covered police courts.

He's been a postcard collector for about 10 years. He gets his memorabilia from other collectors or at shows where dealers "buy and sell history" as Harry puts it.

He was telling me that there's a big difference between a collector and a speculator. "Anyone who just sells off all his items for whatever price isn't a collector. He's a speculator," he said. "There are some things I have that I wouldn't part with for any price."

Almost all of Harry's cards are what used to be called "penny postcards". As I recall, they were a penny to buy and a penny to post.

At the time I saw him, there was one card he really wanted to get for his collection. It was a postcard of Newtonville. That's a little village between Newcastle and Port Hope. Harry said he'd give his shirt to get a card of Newtonville. He confided that he knew a collector who had one, but wouldn't sell it for love nor money.

Harry understood. He's a collector himself — not a speculator.

Organic Gamble

❧

People who go with the flow of nature know more than the rest of us. Most of us go tearing around in a tinsel world, frenetically searching for the golden fleece of success. We don't see the forest for the trees. As the ancients would put it, we're like a man riding an ox looking for an ox.

But every once in a while, you meet people who seem to work without working, who move with an easy rhythm, who seem to live effortlessly yet creatively.

Some are born with such a gift. Others, like the Pronk family who farm near Beaverton, had to learn it.

For 27 years they operated in the usual modern way, using pesticides and chemical compounds to control their land and feed their livestock.

But five years ago, they gambled. They switched over to organic farming!

To neighbouring farmers, it looked like a foolhardy gamble. To hard-nosed, died-in-the-wool scientific types, it sounded like pie-in-the-sky nonsense. Others looked upon the Pronks with a mixture of curiosity and scepticism.

Nevertheless, the Pronks went into action. They converted manure into compost and spread it on their 300 acres of land where they grow grain and hay. They gave chemical-free feed to their 150 head of Holsteins.

They started a new chemical-free vegetable and herb garden. Agnes, the mother of the family, now makes bread, cheese, soup, muffins and yogurt all from the farm produce.

She and her husband Bert, along with their oldest son Murray, are partners in the enterprise. They're always on the move in a relaxed sort of way. And they smile a lot.

Bert, who came from Holland as a youth, still has a trace of an accent.

"It's the best thing we ever did," said Bert. "We're saving on the cost of fertilizer, but even more important, we really enjoy farming now."

"I feel close to nature for the first time," added his son Murray. "It's an experiment that completely changed our lives."

We walked out to their small orchard. Six inches of compost were packed at the base. The trunks had been painted with lime, compost and clay. The trees looked healthy. So did the Pronks.

They aren't alone in their new methods. There's been a dramatic increase in organic farming even in the past year. Currently, there are about 25,000 acres under organic cultivation in Ontario alone.

Recently, the family held an open house. To their surprise, there were close to 400 visitors. Some of the farmers who arrived came back later for a second look.

One thing is sure. Where organic farming is concerned, nobody's laughing anymore.

Deer Unlimited

❦

Like most of us, I'm always happily surprised when a deer suddenly appears on the side of a highway. They're one of nature's most beautiful and graceful creatures. Usually, they gaze at you briefly with wide-eyed curiosity, and then lope away into a nearby bush.

But imagine seeing well over 1,000 of them browsing, running, and frolicking in a 57-acre yard — some of them wandering over to say hello.

It wasn't at some huge wildlife preserve in a faraway country. It was among the rolling hills up Moonstone way, south of Orillia.

They were red deer from New Zealand, brought here as breeding stock by John Bradley and four partners. The reddish-tinged deer will be sold to farmers who want to start their own deer farms.

The deer were farm-bred in New Zealand which has more than a million head grazing in fenced pastures. They were air-lifted in groups by cargo-jet from Auckland. It's a multi-million dollar project — a joint venture between the Canadian partners and New Zealander Tim Willis, who introduced deer farming to his native country 40 years ago.

While we watched the deer, Bradley, a 29-year-old farmer and entrepreneur, was telling me that in the early days, Tim Willis was concerned the New Zealand deer might become an endangered species. He began capturing them in the wild by leaping on their backs from a helicopter and wrestling them to the ground. They formed the nucleus of his first deer herd.

"Most farm-bred venison purchased in North America today is imported from New Zealand," said Jim, "but the demand exceeds the supply. Willis persuaded us to start this project."

He went on to say that venison is growing in popularity because it is lower in cholesterol and fat, and higher in protein than any other red meat.

Bradley and his partners call their company Goldstream Deer Grove and sell the deer at $2,500 a head. Apparently, deer are far easier to care for than other livestock, but require higher fences.

"It's an ideal replacement for tobacco fields and grapevines which have been forced out of production," said Jim.

I told him I'd pass the word along to some of my farmer buddies around places like Delhi and Niagara.

Herb Haven

❦

It's a connoisseur's delight. A culinary cornucopia. In a huge greenhouse complex in the village of Goodwood is Canada's largest collection of herbs. There are over 500 varieties, each one identified in detail.

Richter Herbs was the country's first gardening centre devoted exclusively to herbs. It's owned by Otto and Waltraut Richter whose love of herbs goes back to their childhood in Austria.

The greenhouses contain a panorama of greenery and exude a freshness and fragrance that only nature's unseen alchemists can provide.

The Richters' work in their hobby. They're in the greenhouses 12 to 14 hours a day explaining to people the nature and uses of herbs and supervising shipments going coast to coast and down into the United States.

Waltraut is a tiny, vibrant woman in her seventies whose blue eyes brighten as she tells you of the variations and values of her beloved herbs. She's neither a doctor nor a herbalist, yet is a much sought after speaker for lectures, demonstrations and seminars.

"I know what herbs can do medicinally because I've seen the

results time after time," she says. "And I learned how to use them for cooking in my mother's kitchen."

You don't see any chemicals at Richters. They have good bugs to eat the bad bugs, and the purism of organic farming is evident everywhere.

The couple started their business as a garden centre in the '60s. At first, they grew a general gardening line and cultivated a few herbs for their own use.

"Although herbs have been used in the Orient and Europe for thousands of years," said Waltraut, "during the flower child era there was a herbal renaissance on this continent. We began to see that our customers were more interested in the herbs we were growing than the other plants. So we switched over to herbs exclusively."

A few years ago, Otto hit upon an ingenious invention. He calls it "Potmaker". It's a simple little wooden gadget for making your own starter pots out of newspaper. It transforms a strip of newspaper into a surprisingly strong starter pot. Seedlings can be transplanted without removing them from the paper. The paper decomposes as the roots grow through it.

Apparently, more and more people are learning the uses of herbs and acquiring more knowledge about them. But to the Richters, herbs are an old story. They've been close to them since they were knee high to a comfrey plant. And appropriately, they even named one of their four sons "Herb".

Sidesaddle Lady

❦

I thought riding sidesaddle was a thing of the past, except for occasional glimpses I've had of the Queen riding her horse sidesaddle at ceremonial events.

But what was once the riding style for women in days gone by, is still alive in the Guelph area where Lois Beecroft teaches it. Lois is known as "The Sidesaddle Lady", and is not only a teacher, but has a rare collection of sidesaddle memorabilia.

Attired in a typical riding habit of yesteryear, with long skirt, matching jacket, frilled blouse and hat with a veil, we watched her step up from a small ladder, slip into the sidesaddle and ride her horse "Alex" down a wooded lane.

A moment later she returned so we could take pictures in an effort to capture the elegance and grace of the manner of riding in Victoria days and earlier eras.

Her fascination with the sidesaddle began in the late seventies while she was an instructor with the Golden Triangle Remedial Riding Program. One 10-year-old student's disabilities made it impossible for her to ride astride. Apart from not riding at all, the only answer was for her to ride sidesaddle.

From that one experience, Lois's career blossomed. Now she gives lessons, clinics, lectures, demonstrations and displays. She's also a collector of riding habits and sidesaddles.

One of the riding habits she has is thought to have been worn by a member of the Eaton family. Lois makes her own habits as well. One skirt she made measures a full 27 feet around the bottom.

Her sidesaddle collection includes a few made around 1800. All have women's names. One called the "Mary-Jo" was made in Calgary in 1905.

Along with everything else in the collection are old stirrups, showing their evolution from the 1830s. Then there's her library of books on the subject. Leafing through them, I learned that sidesaddles have been in use since the 1600s, and that Ann of Bohemia first brought the idea to England.

Lois says that when women riders put on the old-fashioned habits, they sense a transformation, as if strolling through a time warp.

"Once they've learned the basics," says Lois. "They find sidesaddle a very comfortable way to ride."

"And invariably," she adds with a smile, "they get a feeling of elegance."

My Finest Hour

❦

I had a brief moment of glory when I made an appearance on the stage of the famed Stratford Festival Theatre!

It was the pinnacle of my entire theatrical career which consists of a couple of high school plays.

But there I was, in my best Shakespearean style booming out, "The fault, dear Brutus, lies not in the stars, but in ourselves that we are underlings." It was my finest hour!

The occasion was a TV news item I was doing about Mervyn "Butch" Blake, Canada's oldest working actor, who was on stage with me as we did a humorous introduction for the item.

"Butch", as he is known by his colleagues (and what he prefers to be called), was 80 years of age! He was still going strong and had just completed his 32nd season with the world-renowned Stratford company. And that year he also completed the "canon". That is, he had acted in all of Shakespeare's 37 plays.

I met "Butch" some years before when I went to Stratford to do a story about superstitions in the theatre.

I had chosen March 15th, what was called "The Ides of March" on the Roman calendar, to do the story. That was the day Julius Caesar was assassinated, and is now considered an unlucky day by theatre people.

Another unlucky thing among actors is whistling backstage. The only way to dispel the curse if you are foolish enough to whistle, is to walk out of the room, turn around three times and then go back in again. I think that's it.

A further unlucky move is to say the name "Macbeth" out loud. Actors refer to it as "that Scottish play". Apparently, many who have done the play seem to run into streaks of bad luck later on. I don't think theatre people take it all too seriously, but some pretend they do. Anyway, "Butch" had a twinkle in his eye as we talked about these omens of ill-fortune.

He's a rather short, stocky man with a well-trimmed white beard and infectious smile. He positively bristles with enthusiasm. As an actor, you can imagine him playing everyone from King Lear to Moses.

My visit was to talk about his career in the theatre which had spanned almost 60 years. It ranges from England's Stratford-on-Avon, where he worked with the likes of Lawrence Olivier and Vivien Leigh, to the Stratford Festival, where he's been on stage with greats like Maggie Smith and William Hutt. He's known, loved and admired by the youngest apprentices to the famous names.

Will he be back next season? Likely. Old actors never die. They just keep on playing roles, perhaps even right into eternity.

Mug Shots

❦

In a converted old schoolhouse on the outskirts of the Georgian Bay village of Stayner, potter Michael Leishman turns out hundreds of mugs a year. They're all the same shape and size and hold 24 oz. of whatever you want to pour into them.

It sounds like a monotonous task. But it's not. Each mug has a face on it. Michael sculpts caricatures of people on the mugs from photographs they leave with him. Mug shots. They cost $50 each, and he can't keep up with the demand.

His unusual craft has brought some caustic comments from his former fellow students at the Ontario College of Art. Leishman is quite capable of doing fine art, but decided to forego the "starving artist" route and take a more materialistic approach.

"In art school we would make ridiculous objects. We would make vaselike things with no holes. If it isn't useful, what good is it?" he comments.

He varies his work to make the occasional cookie jar with a face on it. And he's been commissioned to make life-size figures for use as mascots in bars and restaurants. When we were there, he was working on the figure of a mermaid which was going to be in an indoor swimming pool. But these items are the gravy. Leishman's bread and butter business is making mugs. His wife, Connie, helps him with it.

I watched them as Michael threw the mugs on a wheel and then let them harden. After that, Leishman picked up one to begin sculpting a caricature. He makes no sketches. He glances at the photographs from time to time, and gradually the resemblance begins to unfold. He worked my own angular face on a mug, and I chuckled as he put on the finishing touches.

Leishman has learned that one of the important ingredients in a happy, fulfilling life is a sense of humour. He doesn't take himself or his work too seriously. He has no regrets about not pursuing a career in fine art. He regards it as more important to put a smile on somebody's mug.

Ghost Town

❦

I got an eerie feeling when I first saw Depot Harbour. It's a "ghost town". It's not down in Nevada or some place like that. It's just out of Parry Sound on the shores of Southern Georgian Bay.

Somehow you don't think of Ontario as having ghost towns. But there are hundreds of them, and Ron Brown, a geographer and writer, probably knows as much about them as anybody.

Ron and I have met a few times, and we have something in common. We both write books about Ontario and have the same publisher. Ron writes stories about the past, while mine are mostly about the present.

It was Ron who took me to see Depot Harbour, which happened to be the particular ghost town that set him off 25 years ago on a search for other deserted and forlorn old places around the province.

As I recall, it took us about 10 minutes to get to the area from Parry Sound. We drove along a highway in Ron's panel truck, then cut off and went down a lane. Dense forests lined the lane.

Suddenly, we came upon a maze of scattered ruins. I stared in disbelief. I had expected the kind of ghost town you see in Western movies. But this looked more like the remnants of ancient Rome. There was a ramshackle curved stone structure that had once been a railway roundhouse. It was partly concealed by the re-advancing forest. Nearby, concrete sidewalks had buckled and heaved. Beside them were rusting fire hydrants. Huge maples still lined the streets, shading rows of foundations. In the distance, there was one house still standing.

"This is Canada's largest freshwater natural harbour," said Ron as we looked out on the Bay. "At the turn of the century, this place was a focal point for rail and shipping."

He showed me pictures he had brought along. There were photos of stores, houses, grain elevators, a big hotel, even the old round house as it existed in the glory days.

But time took its toll on the Depot Harbour. In the late twenties and thirties the town fell apart. The railway pulled out, fire destroyed major buildings and people left for employment elsewhere. Houses were demolished, and the wood was carted away to be used to build cottages around Parry Sound.

But here's an ironic twist: Some months later, I met a man in a downtown Toronto restaurant who said, "I've got a great story for you. We've just moved to a ghost town called Depot Harbour. We fixed up the only remaining house there, and we're going to have a few neighbours who are building near us."

He seemed very proud of his new-found home. And why not? It's not everybody who can live in a legitimate, bona fide ghost town.

Pyramid Power

❦

You may have heard of "pyramid power". It was in the news some years ago when Red Kelly, who was the coach of the Toronto Maple Leafs at the time, was said to be trying pyramid power to prop up the sagging Leafs. As I recall, it didn't do much good.

But Bill and Betty Drevnick, a couple of energetic seniors who live in the village of Combermere in northeastern Ontario, may have better luck.

They've constructed a huge pyramid-shaped greenhouse said to be the largest in the country where they hope to grow giant vegetables using energy that pyramids are supposed to attract.

Bill and Betty were neighbours of a man named Les Brown who was convinced the ancient Egyptians knew something we didn't know. He wrote books and gave lectures all over the world on the power of the pyramid.

"Les Brown believed that pyramids take energy from the North Pole, the South Pole, radio waves and so on, and concentrate it," said Betty. "We saw quite a bit of him before he died, and a few years ago we decided to see if his ideas on growing vegetables really worked."

The Drevnicks started with a few small greenhouse pyramids in their backyard. They found that the strawberries they grew in them were much larger than those they grew in a nearby field.

Then a few years ago, they began to build the big pyramid. Bill, who has worked in the bush all his life and is now in his mid-seventies, hauled spruce logs from the forest, and with the help of his son, Charles, erected a frame. A special weather-resistant plastic was put over it. The result is a pyramid 50 feet high with five growing levels. Each side is 78 feet long.

When we were there the whole ground floor was filled with strawberry plants. Only a few berries had appeared, but Betty showed us some leaves that were about 6 1/2 inches long.

"In the past," said Betty, "the berries in the small pyramids were not only much larger, but juicier. So we're hoping for the best."

The Drevnicks were saying that just standing inside the pyramid has an effect on some people.

"We've had visitors tell us it makes them feel serene," said Betty, "but others say they feel uncomfortable and nervous."

We didn't feel anything in particular until we walked up the wooden stairs to the fifth level. It was 104° up there. We felt hot! Pyramid power had nothing to do with it.

Totem Poles

❦

For three generations, the Whetung family have operated a general store at Crowe's Landing in the Kawartha Lakes district.

The store hasn't changed much since the early days except for several totem poles that have been erected recently around the property. There are four poles on the porch of the store, three on a lawn and one down at the family's marina, a few hundred yards away.

Don and Lois Whetung now own the place. Their 26-year-old son, Brent, carved the totem poles over the past few years. I talked to him down at the marina while he was carving another one and asked him how he happened to become involved in the work.

"Four years ago I met one of my grandfather's friends who was an expert carver," he said, "and for the first time became really aware of my heritage. He explained native ways and beliefs and how they are expressed in the symbolism of totem poles."

Brent went on to say he began to look around and discovered that although carving totem poles is still common out west, the craft has almost died out in Ontario. He decided to try to revive it. He learned basic carving from his grandfather's friend, studied native lore, and went to work.

He took a break from the carving, and we walked up to the store while he told me the meaning of the figures carved on one of the poles outside.

"You always read the symbols from the bottom upward," said Brent. He pointed to the snake he had carved at the bottom of the pole. "The snake represents the spirit of evil. The thunderbird above it is a sign of power over evil, and the eagle at the top symbolizes strength and freedom."

As is traditional with Ojibwa carvers, Brent features birds, animals and their relationship to the spiritual world. Like some of the other totem poles I've seen, there's an aura of mystery and grandeur about his work.

His father is his greatest fan, and although he knows nothing about carving, understands the symbolism and is happy to explain it to visitors.

Brent has done 15 of the impressive carvings. He's sold some of them, but doesn't care if he sells them or not. Not only that, he doesn't sell them to just anyone. As he puts it, they have to be "in tune with the totem".

Venerable Vehicles

❦

One day, I went for a ride in a car that's a year older than I am. It was a 1914 Ford, and despite its advanced years, was as perky as a Porsche. The driver was Peter Fawcett who, with his partner Art Carty, operates the Fawcett Motor Carriage Co. in Whitby. They restore antique and late model automobiles and are one of just a handful of Ontario companies that are in the business full-time.

We roared down Brock Street at maybe 20 m.p.h. The wind

whipped my scarf and I hung onto my hat. I guess we didn't really roar down the street. It was more of a chug-chug. But a fast chug-chug.

When we got back to the garage, I took a closer look at some of the other old cars. The garage is a rambling affair with a nostalgic appeal. We watched one of the shop's four craftsmen restoring a 1910 McGlaughlin Buick touring car. It had been retrieved from a junk yard and was being rebuilt from scratch. Sitting near it was a similar car in mint condition. It had been made in 1910 in nearby Oshawa by Sam McGlaughlin's General Motors of Canada. They were using it as a model in the restoration of the other car.

Peter took us around to see some of the many restored classic automobiles. There were about 40 in a barn beside the garage, but they have hundreds in a lot a few miles from the shop waiting to be returned to their former glory.

Prospective buyers were coming into the barn. One young man was looking closely at a 1934 Cadillac. It was priced at $40,000. There was also a 1928 Model A Ford selling for $19,000. Quite a variety.

The company was started by Peter's father 20 years ago. Peter grew up with the place. And his partner, Art, who lived a few doors from the shop, used to spend almost all of his spare time working around there, until he finally bought into the business.

Peter and Art have restored cars that once belonged to famous figures like Babe Ruth and boxing great Jack Dempsey. Dempsey's car was a Kissel Speedster. Only two are known to exist.

They're always booked weeks in advance at the shop. They love the old cars and seem to be able to perform mechanical miracles with them. They have a way of turning bits and pieces into classic masterpieces.

Sleeping Children

❦

Although it's been around for a number of years, I'd never heard of an organization called SCAW until recently. The letters stand for Sleeping Children Around the World.

SCAW provides "bedkits" for children in Third World countries. The kits include a bedroll, ground sheet, pillow, blanket, two pairs of pyjamas, a towel, sweater, pants and one or two T-shirts. All are purchased in the country where the child lives to save transportation costs, and help the local economy.

Last year alone, 12,000 children from Calcutta to Ecuador received a warm bed and pyjamas — for the first time in their lives. Most have never met Murray Dryden, the man responsible for their good night's sleep.

Dryden, 78, the father of National Hockey League goalies Ken and David, became a man with a mission 17 years ago while visiting Pakistan. He was shocked at the sight of children sleeping on roadsides.

When he returned to his home in Islington, the retired construction executive put his tremendous energies into starting SCAW. Since then, a network of volunteers have helped him raise over two million dollars for bedkits!

People send $28 per child which pays for one kit. As each child receives a bed, a photo is taken with a card identifying the donor who provided the kit. The picture is later sent to the donor.

The whole operation is run mostly from a big room on the second floor of Dryden's home. We watched about 15 volunteers addressing envelopes, making out receipts, sending out photos and innumerable details involved in such work.

SCAW is unique in more ways than one. It's thought to be the only organization of its kind in the world and amazingly not one penny has ever been spent for administration costs — not even postage! Dryden pays for everything himself!

Murray and the volunteers travel the world at their own expense to see that the kits reach their proper destinations. None of them claim tax exemptions, although donors can write off their contributions. By the way, the address is:

Murray Dryden
28 Pinehurst Crescent
ETOBICOKE, Ontario M9A 3A5
Phone (416) 231-1841

Cheques should be made out to SCAW.

As Murray says, "People sleep better knowing they just put a child to bed."

The Steamers

🍃

Steam locomotives — those cross-country workhorses of yesteryear — are still huffing and puffing their way around the Whitchurch Highlands Railway near the village of Ballantrae.

Ballantrae, north of Markham, isn't very big. Neither is the railway line. Neither are the locomotives. They're scale models of the real thing, but only about three feet high and four feet long. Nevertheless, hot coal beds stoke up the engines and blast steam into the pistons. After picking up their cars at the car barns, the little trains can carry a full load of 12 passengers!

The railway, which has about a quarter mile of track, runs through a forested area of scenic beauty. I took a trip on a train operated by John Vincent. We went tearing around at about three miles an hour across a small bridge, past the diminutive car barns, over a couple more bridges and back to the tiny station where other passengers were waiting.

The rail line is run by a group of hobbyists called the Richmond Hill Live Steamers. There are 40 members in the club, and on weekends some of them are always on hand to share with others their enthusiasm for the steam age.

They don't just operate the trains. They build them. After I'd taken my trip, John took me back to the basement workshop at his home in Markham. It was here that he had spent four years constructing the locomotive that had pulled us. To me, the workshop was a maze of complex machinery. John showed me the plans for another scale locomotive he was making. I got the general idea, then we drove back to the site.

John showed me how the miniature water tower worked, and the small switches near the station. Two trains were in operation and Bernie Sherman, one of the members had been delegated as switchman for the day.

Like so many small boys, both John and Bernie had been fascinated by trains when youngsters. But unlike most of us, their interest continued into later years, and ultimately to the complex business of creating the locomotives from scratch.

So steam locomotives are still alive and well, thanks to the skill and enthusiasm of aficionados of the steam era. Men who love to ride the rails, and bring joy to the hearts of kids of all ages.

The Farm

❦

Jack de Wit has an interesting farm near the village of Brooklin, north of Whitby. Simply called "The Farm", hundreds of young schoolchildren visit it every year to see livestock in a natural setting.

It's not a model farm with the latest in equipment and all the rest of it. True, the rambling farmhouse built in 1858 has been designated a heritage building, and the old barn has been there since 1877, but other than that, it's a very average-looking farm.

And that's the whole idea. It's not supposed to be a showplace. It's just to give the very young an idea of how domestic animals live and are cared for in most small farms. The major difference is that "The Farm" is a top-flight agricultural classroom!

Jack and his assistant, Monica Taylor, don't just show the children around. They ask questions. They answer questions. It's a give and take educational experience.

How to milk a goat was one of the projects on the tour. Jack gave a demonstration, then a six-year-old boy took a run at it. I expected him to botch it completely, but he did surprisingly well. Then Jack asked what the milk was used for. He's a born teacher. He doesn't merely give facts, he draws out the answers. One thing I learned was that aside from making cheese and ice cream, you can also make soap out of the milk.

Some of the kindergarten crowd met "Rambo", the friendly bull calf. Others saw their winter woollies on the hoof, and some shorn sheep in among those who still have their fleece.

Monica took over while I talked to Jack for a few minutes. "You'd be surprised," he said, "how little many kids know about fundamentals. A lot of them think milk comes from Becker's and meat from the A&P."

When we went back to join the others at the chicken coop, there were squeals of delight as some reached in to take eggs right from the nest. It was another new experience for most of them.

The most popular feature came at the end of the tour. The boundless energy of childhood was released in the hayloft. There were ropes where the kids could swing to their heart's content, and go flying off into the hay.

About 5,000 children a year visit Jack's place to get a true picture of a few aspects of life down on the farm. I suppose to a child who has been brought up in the country, they're all just ordinary things of life as time goes by. But to an inner city kid "The Farm" is a real eye-opener.

Stuntgirl

❦

Dawn Hallson is a stunt girl. We met over coffee in her hometown of Cookstown where she was visiting her parents. She appeared to be a diminutive fragile girl. So much for appearances. Dawn has been to a school of hard knocks, otherwise known as Stunt Productions in Toronto. She'll do anything required for her work in TV and movies. That includes setting herself on fire, throwing herself downstairs or off a bridge, jumping out a window, or even being dragged behind a car.

I couldn't imagine this slip of a girl doing such things. But at her parents' home, we saw her in action. She had changed from a flowered dress she had been wearing into old jeans and an old sweater. Under that was padding, so she didn't look quite as fragile.

Terry took pictures of her falling down a long staircase. It was frightening, but we'd seen others at work at the stunt school and knew that the stunts were carefully planned and that injuries were few and far between.

We went out on the road and saw Dawn hanging halfway out of the passenger's seat of a fast-moving car. Her feet were in the car, the rest of her dragging on the pavement. Finally, she slipped off and was left lying on the road. The car sped off. It was just like you see in the movies or on TV. In fact, Dawn has done the stunt on the popular Street Legal and three other Canadian productions.

The car was driven by her husband Rick. He's a big, tall, young man who's program director of a Barrie radio station.

"She has more guts than any man I know. She's absolutely fearless. I never worry about her being injured. I've seen the training and there isn't much left to chance," he told me.

Dawn is still waiting for her big break — if you'll pardon the expression under such circumstances. She may have to go to California to get it, but will still live in Canada.

She loves stunt work. "I was always a wild one as a kid. Always a tomboy. I'd climb out on the end of tree branches and all that sort of stuff. Now I can do all the things my mother told me not to do," she laughed.

The Ice Man

❦

I have happy childhood memories of our ice man. He was a big jolly man, and when he'd come down the street with his team of horses pulling a cart filled with blocks of ice, we'd run out to greet him. On a hot summer day, there was nothing, absolutely nothing, like a chunk of cooling ice.

When the cart stopped in front of the various houses on his route, the ice man would jump down, and with heavy iron tongs, haul out a big block of ice. Then he'd lug it to the customer's kitchen and ease it into their ice box.

Meanwhile, the neighbourhood kids would gather round the back of the cart and grab some of the pieces of ice that the ice man used to chop off for us. Later, our family moved away and I never saw the ice man again. Electrical refrigerators arrived and I guess the traditional ice men were no longer needed.

But in London one day, I met a bona fide ice man of the old school, as was his father before him. Now in his seventies, Harold Cushman has been an ice man for 55 years and is still at it, although these days he delivers packs of ice cubes to convenience stores and supermarkets for North Star Ice. It's a small company, but the only one of its kind in the London Area

The owner, Ross Snibert, started the firm 25 years ago and along the way became quite an authority on the history of the ice industry. All sorts of ancient ice tongs and hundreds of old ice picks line the walls of the outer office. There's a photographic history of ice harvesting on London's Thames River, and a picture of Harold's father standing beside his horses and cart in 1910.

"My father had a team of blind horses," Harold recalls. "They knew every house to go to on the route."

He says the first ice truck appeared on London streets in 1929, and the last year ice was cut from the river was 1924.

Talking to Harold brought back a flood of memories, and I drove off happy in the knowledge that not all of the ice men of yesteryear had just melted away.

Border Collies

It is interesting to watch sheepdogs in action. Especially top flight types like Border Collies that have been born and bred to herd livestock.

Jim Clark, whose family has operated a farm near Blenheim for five generations, began breeding Border Collies as a sideline several years ago. Now they take up most of his time.

Clark travels across Canada, down to the States and to the British Isles for sheepdog trials. Mostly with Mirk, Moss and Kate, three of his most talented dogs.

They're the traditional type of dog, first bred on the English and Scottish borders over a century ago. Mirk and Moss were trained in the Old Country, but Jim trained Kate himself.

We caught up with Jim and his collies at the Blenheim farm. They were "between engagements" as they say in show business, taking a breather from the trials and demonstrations.

Terry had been looking forward to taking shots of the dogs in action. He's filmed in various parts of the world, and one of his favourite clips is one he did of dogs herding sheep on the Scottish Moors.

As soon as Jim and the dogs went to work Terry began following them with his camera.

Jim had brought out his small herd of Scottish Blackface sheep. They scampered around until he began to give both voice and whistle commands to the dogs. The commands vary for each dog.

Two short blasts and a long one tell a dog to head counter-clockwise. We saw Kate dash out in a long arc in front of the sheep. Another blast and Kate crouched gazing at the sheep. The dogs control the sheep with eye contact. The sheep shy away from the dog's gaze. After a series of commands and manoeuvres the dogs herded the sheep back to Jim, and then to the barn.

Later, we went over to the farmhouse. Jim's wife, Ruth, was showing Jenny the latest litter of puppies. They were just 10 days old, but in the months to come they would begin training for their life's work.

The Clarks were telling us that the dog's herding instincts are so strong that they can herd children into a schoolyard.

Even more surprising, if a group of people are in a room and the dogs happen to be there, the Border Collies feel uncomfortable unless the people are bunched together.

Spike Art

One day artist Tom King was walking along an abandoned railway track near his cottage on Lake Chemong in the Peterborough district.

He reached down and picked up a battered old railroad spike. He looked at it carefully. As he continued walking he picked up a few more, and an idea began to shape in his mind.

He went back to his studio and made a few rough sketches. It was the beginning of what could be "Spike Art".

The sketches he drew were of angular figures that he turned into small sculptured pieces made of the railroad spikes.

He took them to a craft show and sold all of them. People had never seen anything quite like them.

King had worked in metal for quite some time, but never had turned out anything with such immediate appeal.

They appear to be simple enough to construct. The figures are of such things as a baseball player at bat, a gardener with his wheelbarrow, a violinist and a saxophone player.

They're about 10 inches tall and weigh around 3 pounds. The bodies of the little people consist of spikes and the accessories are formed from rods, wires and pieces of scrap metal.

But making them is not as simple as it may appear. It takes Tom 12 hours or more to make a single figure.

He brushes and grinds each spike to clean it, then heats and fashions it in his forge to human shape. Welding on parts, sanding and coating with rust-proofing are final steps.

Each figure is unique because it bears the hammer marks and dents it had when it was a railroad spike. Tom makes no attempt to remove the signs of its origins.

Each is copyrighted and guaranteed to be a limited edition. He makes only 100 in each series. The figures sell for between $65 and $150 depending on the work involved.

He gets the spikes where railroad lines are being pulled out. He buys two or three pails at a time from demolition contractors.

As we watched him at work I was thinking that mankind's ingenuity and imagination seems to know no bounds. Artist King seems to have hit the nail on the head with his idea as he hammers home his unusual and intriguing bits of artistry.

Scissors Art

❧

Lini Grol is a beautiful 76-year-old woman with a bear-trap mind and talents expressed in works of artistry that flow from the heart.

She paints in oils, does some sculpture, writes books of poetry and prose, but is likely best known for her scissors art.

The closest I've ever come to this type of art work was at the tender age of three when I took a run at my mother's lace curtains with a pair of scissors. As I recall, my artistic efforts along these lines were abruptly and rather violently terminated.

Lini Grol's cutting career took a different twist. Although she began to study the ancient art of scissors cutting when she was a child in her native Holland, it was along more intricate, creative lines.

Today, when you enter her studio in the Niagara Peninsula village of Fonthill, you see magnificent pictures hanging on the walls that appear to be India ink drawings at first glance. But they've all been cut from sheets of paper with a simple pair of scissors.

There are cuttings of birds, animals, flowers, trees and trailing vines that have been pasted on backgrounds of heavy paper or cloth.

One of her award-winning works depicts the Indian legend of "The Maid of the Mist". Many others have to do with family life — a mother and child, a couple and their baby, or similar portrayals.

"I'm an admirer and lover of family life," she says. "It's the building block of society and I do anything I can to further it in my scissor cutting, poems and books."

Her productivity has been enormous. Her works have been displayed at innumerable shows. Buyers from other countries have taken them back to their homelands and she has established herself as a creative artist on an international scale.

Lini is quick-witted, knowledgeable, with an aura of tranquillity and wisdom characteristic of true philosophers of life. Her depth of feeling is reflected in her scissors art.

It's a 2000-year-old craft and Lini carries on the tradition with her unusual gifts. It's quite amazing when you consider that she draws no designs. She cuts the paper freehand. In this intriguing art form, the artist's brushes are simply the scissors.

Quadeville Quartz

Rockhounds are an interesting bunch. They're collectors of minerals. Some are professionals who buy and sell stones and gems. But most are hobbyists who are only too happy to introduce you to a whole new world. The one under your feet.

We meet them in surprising places. One summer evening, Jenny and I were strolling out on the pier at Port Dover and met a young Japanese rockhound who wondered why we had never done a story about the Wal-Gem mine in Quadeville. He waxed eloquently about the mine. "It has the largest deposit of rose quartz in North America," he enthused.

Jenny made a note of it, and one October day when she was cleaning out her purse the note fluttered down like a falling leaf.

About a week later, we were on our way to Quadeville which turned out to be a little village in the Ottawa Valley, sixty miles east of Bancroft.

We wound our way along a country road to the site. The mine itself was a rockhound's dream come true. But we found the couple who own it, Don and Fran McKay, just as interesting.

Their backgrounds were the stuff that novels are made of. At one time Don was a Shakespearean actor in his native England. He did some theatre work when he came to Canada, but for a while was involved in mining, among other things, and later became a newsman for the old Toronto Telegram and The Globe and Mail. While in mining he became an avid rockhound.

Fran had a varied career. At one point she was a cocktail waitress at the Desert Inn in Las Vegas where she met and married a man named McCoy who owned the Wal-Gem mine.

She came back with him to live in the rambling lodge near the mine. Within a few years she became a knowledgeable rockhound and a skilled jewellery maker.

When her husband died she thought she'd have to sell the mine. She couldn't be showing people around, turning out jewellery and go on by herself.

Then she met Don at one of the many rockhound gatherings, and it was love at first sight! Shortly after, they were married and Don came to help her with the mine.

The four of us hit it off right away. Being newspapermen of the same era, Don and I talked of mutual buddies from our Press Club days and Jenny was absorbed in watching Fran make a pendant in the adjacent workshop.

Later, we strolled over to the mine and I gathered enough material to write a TV script. Terry arrived the next day. So did two reporters from area papers who were there to do a story about us. Bella and Debbie, a couple of neighbours, came over. I worked them into the script and the whole thing became an enjoyable, at times, hilarious event.

Terry caught everything on camera. The reporters, John and Scott, were shooting pictures and all of us, including the magnificent rose quartz, were all smiles in the autumn sunlight.

We're going back to see Don and Fran again sometime. When we do I'll get down to business and write a story about the mine itself, which I intended to do in the first place, but got carried away — sidetracked. Jenny says I do it all the time.

Joe's Hidden Talent

❦

By nature, native people sense certain things more than the rest of us do. They lived in harmony with nature for centuries. They have a built-in mystical spirituality unique to their race.

As time went on they had to straddle two worlds. One foot in the land of the teepee, the other sunk in the metallic glitter of technology.

Many of them forgot their culture, their identification with the earth, creatures of the forests and crystal-clear streams uprooted in the march of the bulldozers gutting their way across the land.

Some of them have rediscovered their heritage and expressed it in native art. Stone sculptor Joseph Jacobs is one of them. And Jacobs' story is as strange as the timeless legends he portrays in stone.

Jacobs is famous now. His work is in the House of Commons and other such places. He's received an honourary doctorate from Trent University for his contribution to native art. One of his small pieces of Iroquois sculpture will sell in the thousands.

But until he was in his mid-thirties, he was totally unaware that he had any artistic talent whatsoever. He still doesn't look upon himself as a "real artist". He's had no training. He doesn't understand how or why his work has had such a powerful influence on the public and other artists. He regards it all as a fluke of fate.

We spent a day with Jacobs at the huge Whetung Ojibwa Crafts and Art Gallery on the Curve Lake Reserve near Peterborough.

He's artist-in-residence there and works in a small cottage not far from the main gallery. We watched him for a while as he carved into rough stone. Eventually he began to tell us of the mosaic of events leading up to the abrupt discovery of his talent and even of his own people.

Joe is a slight man with sharp features. He speaks of himself hesitantly as if groping for words to describe his feelings.

"I was a construction worker. It was all I'd ever done," he began. "But after a fall from a building I was hospitalized with injuries that meant I could never work again. I thought I was through. There didn't seem much point in living. I couldn't support my family."

Then one day his nephew came to see him and brought him a chisel and a piece of stone to pass the time away.

He began to carve, and what was in his mind appeared in the stone. He was shocked. He continued to carve daily and began studying books on Indian mythology until he was steeped in the lore of his forefathers.

"Everything in the universe fell into place for me," he said. "It was like a miracle."

We walked over to the gallery where his work was on display. Jenny and Terry who are both talented artists, stopped to look at a complex carving called "The Discovery of Fire".

I wandered off to look at some paintings. When I returned the two of them were still looking at the mystical saga that Jacobs had caused to burst into being.

"All of the parts seem to float together," said Jenny.

I looked more carefully. And although I'm not an artist, I understood what she meant.

It Takes All Kinds

❦

It's unlikely that you've ever heard of the village of Cherry Hill, and even more unlikely you've heard of the Reptile Breeding Foundation.

But zoologists the world over know of them. Cherry Hill is a little place down near the Bay of Quinte, and the Reptile

Breeding Foundation is a unique centre dedicated to the preservation of rare species.

I suppose most of us are repelled by such things as snakes and lizards. But Tom Huff, the director of the Foundation, loves the little critters. He's devoted to them. So are his three associates. They pick up big toads, turtles, snakes, lizards and whatnot, and stroke them with affection, the way we would a dog or a cat.

Tom opened the door of one of the larger pens in the rambling building. I had mixed emotions as a Bengal Monitor Lizard came waddling over toward me, his forked tongue flicking out as he hissed at me.

"He's very territorial and the closest remaining species to dinosaurs. He looks and acts tough, but he's harmless."

Before the tour was over, I had seen an Angel Island Chuckwalla, a Mongolian frog-eyed sand gecko, a Solomon Island prehensile-tailed skink and several other rare reptiles.

From a box in one of the rooms Tom pulled out what looked like a thick rusty-brown snake. "Legless lizard," he said and pointed to the eyelids and ear slits which snakes don't have. It was these harmless lizards that were used for the snake-pit scene in the film "Raiders of the Lost Ark".

Along the way, Tom explained that all of the reptiles had a place in the balance of nature. "They're more than just a pretty face," chuckled Tom as he patted a particularly nasty-looking python.

Wine Cellar

❦

The first wine cellar I ever saw was at Casa Loma. I was just a lad at that time and I remember tagging along behind my mother as we roamed the famed storybook castle with its wide casement windows and tall turrets overlooking the city.

As I recall, the wine cellar was big, dark and dingy. There were heavy-looking casks lining the walls. It was an awesome place and my boyhood imagination conjured up visions of knights shedding their shining armour and retreating to the cellar after a hard day on the battlefield. Or wizards scurrying around, getting wines to add to their magic potions so they'd be more palatable to the unsuspecting.

I mentioned to my mother that it would be nice if we had a castle to live in with lots of rooms, a stable for horses and a wine cellar. She said something like "It's too big and would cost a fortune to heat." It was one of those sensible comments adults always make to dispel wonderful childhood delusions of grandeur. She was right, of course.

But one day, I saw another wine cellar that impressed me in a totally different way. It wasn't very big, and it wasn't damp and dingy. It was a snug wine cellar in the lower floor of a chalet nestled at the foot of the Blue Mountain near Collingwood.

The cellar was stocked with about 2,000 bottles of red wine, white wine, sherry and cider, all of it made by Joanne and Wally Anderson, members of the Blue Mountain Guild of Winemakers.

The Guild was started in 1968 by a few at-home winemakers. There are now 20 members and all of them have their own wine cellars.

You might think that with all that juice of the grape flowing so freely, their monthly meetings could become orgies that would put even old Bacchus and his buddies to shame.

On the contrary, the members take their hobby seriously — very seriously. When they get together, there's some genteel "sipping" or "sampling", but they're more concerned with winemaking techniques and variations of the age-old winemaking processes.

In the early days, when they'd get fermentation fever, they'd stomp bare-footed on the grapes — the traditional way of extracting the juice. Now they have a rotary crusher and wine press. They also have complex equipment to siphon off sediment, and a machine to cork the bottles.

It's another of those interesting hobbies that add spice to life.

And, although some people might not be interested in seeing your stamp collection for example, there aren't too many who would turn down a tour through your wine cellar.

Coffee Club

❦

Each morning historian John Lunau and about 30 of his cronies meet for coffee at the T & T Donuts on Main Street in Markham.

It's not your average coffee club where they shoot the breeze about nothing in particular. They're all historians, and for more than two decades they've been busy gathering dusty old records and made-in-Markham artifacts which they bring to John.

The members range in age from 60 to 86, and in some cases have molded Markham's history themselves. The day I joined them, 84-year-old Reg Kirk had brought along a shovel made in 1825. Another member, Al Shenfield, a former deputy-treasurer of the town, brought a vintage pencil sharpener to add to Lunau's already huge collection of historic items that clutter his 19th century home on 16th Avenue.

His home is just a stone's throw from the Markham Museum which John founded in 1970. He served as curator until 1987. While his "job" may be over, his schedule is just as busy. At 62, he's the youngest of the tightly-knit bunch. Ever since he can remember, Lunau has been interested in history, especially of the town where he was born. The Lunaus have been in Markham since 1794.

"When I was about 12," he says, "I would talk to older residents who were in their 80s and 90s. I'd write down the stories they remembered about Markham's past. Then I began collecting."

He chuckles when he recalls his days as bailiff of York County. "I was able to add to my collection quite considerably. Instead of seizing some historical item, I'd just buy it."

People came from across Canada and the U.S. to consult with Lunau about their ancestors who once lived in the Markham area. Invariably, he has the answers. If by chance he doesn't, one of his buddies can usually come up with a lead.

There's a big board hanging on one of the walls of the donut shop where the club members hang their coffee cups. The cups were donated by the Corning people and each member's initials are engraved on them in 14 karat gold.

There's not much idle gossip at the daily meetings. Oh, the members veer off every once in a while to solve all of the worlds' problems, but primarily Markham's past is the subject of discussion.

So aside from making donuts daily, the little old donut shop is also preserving history every day.

Goats Galore

☙

Goats don't eat tin cans and things like that. They're very fussy about their food. And not all of them are raised for milk or meat.

Up around Coboconk in the north Kawartha Lakes area, there's a family that raises goats for the mohair they provide!

They're Angora goats. They have a woolly-looking fleece, and, at first glance, look like sheep that need a haircut. But those that have been clipped look like any other goats.

Originally from Turkey, the Angoras each produce up to 24 pounds of mohair in a year — a product used in clothing and furniture that now sells at about $5 a pound on the international market.

Angora goats are a relatively new addition to the livestock raised in Ontario. David and Margaret Suckling imported 18 of them from Texas several years ago, and now have a herd of 130, which may be the largest herd in the province.

The goats were a godsend for the Suckling family. They'd left the security of their city jobs in the mid-70s to farm in Kawartha country, although they had absolutely no knowledge of farming.

They wanted to get away from it all. And they sure did. The century-old farmhouse they bought had no heat or water. The wiring ran across the living room floor. They had to start from scratch, learning how to fix machinery, fence fields and manage livestock. It wasn't easy. Especially with fourteen children — some of their own, some adopted. But with the help of the older children they muddled through.

They raised fruits and vegetables. They raised pigs, Angus cattle, chickens, rabbits and sheep to eke out a living.

Then one night about eight years ago, they were watching the news and saw a story we did about a small herd of Angora goats on a farm north of Sudbury. It gave them an idea.

David went down to Texas and bought 18 bloodline goats. When he brought them back, two of the older sons in the family, Chris and Gerry, were delegated to care for them.

Almost overnight they developed a thriving business. This year, the Sucklings will ship about 20 kids to Britain at a selling price of $8,000 each.

The boys also shear and card the mohair for hand spinners, and recently acquired a big mechanical spinner to produce yarn.

We toured the barn to see some of the goats. They're fluffy, very gentle animals.

They have names too. One of the larger bucks is called "Golly". I asked Gerry how they happened to choose such a moniker.

"Well," he laughed, "a good number of the kids are by Golly."

Back In Time Train

❦

One sunny morning in June, I boarded a train in the Lake Erie village of Port Stanley and headed in the direction London. I had picked up a ticket at the railroad station.

The station was as I remembered it when, as a young newsman, I started a weekly paper in the village and used to go up to London to have it printed. That was in the mid-thirties and the train was known as the London and Port Stanley Railway. It was an electric railway and the coaches were big green ones.

But this time was different. There were only two small cars pulled by a little green diesel. It's been running for a few years as a tourist attraction and goes for about three miles. It loafs along to another ancient station — this one at the hamlet of Union. The tiny station looked the same as when I first saw it over half a century ago. We got off for a few minutes and went inside where there were photos of the old L & PS, as the line was called in its glory days.

The excursion train and the memorabilia were all brought together in 1982 by a group of railway buffs. All volunteers, they bought the abandoned track, found the excursion diesel in a scrap yard, and gathered papers and photos from early eras. The original train goes back to 1853. It changed hands several times and in 1915 Sir Adam Beck converted it into an electric railway.

For years it brought land-locked London and St. Thomas travellers down to Lake Erie for a cooling dip and to hear the big bands of the '30s and '40s at Port Stanley's famed Stork Club.

The round trip on the excursion train takes 45 minutes. On the way, I talked to Al Howlett who was living out his dreams as an engineer, and Bob McLean, fulfilling fantasies as a conductor. Al was one of the early members of the group.

"We've only just begun," said Al, "We're buying up regular full-size freight cars and coaches that have been abandoned. We're restoring them and hope to have a train running up as far as St. Thomas. It will have a dining car and everything!" He had a faraway look in his eyes as he gazed along the track.

The enthusiasm of the railroad enthusiasts knows no bounds. They spend almost all year of their spare time working on their restoration project. I watched Dick Walker clearing out debris from a battered old coach. His 13-year-old son Steve was helping him. Father and son teams are not uncommon among the group.

As I recall, the old L & PS was affectionately known as the "Late and Poor Service" by the regulars. But during its heyday, it carried 28 million passengers to and from the picturesque port. And thanks to the efforts of the hustling railroad historians, it appears that the historic old train still hasn't reached the end of the line.

Small World

❦

Some years ago, carpenter and cabinet maker Ted Roberts made a doll house for a neighbour's child as a gift. The little girl loved it, but wondered if he'd make a small bed for it.

Ted, who had never tried his hand at miniature furniture, managed to turn out a little bed modelled on an antique which was among the many pieces of antique furniture he and his wife had collected over the years.

He enjoyed making it and decided to build a few more things for the doll house. He found a couple of tools more adaptable to such meticulous work and, using their antiques as models, made exact replicas in miniature with the use of a micrometer.

Ted became fascinated with making the tiny furniture and now that he's in his mid-70s and retired, he has time to pursue his absorbing hobby.

We visited him at his home in Picton in the Bay of Quinte area. He knew we were coming and had set up a display in the living room. It was a Lilliputian antique shop. Perhaps museum would be a better way to put it.

There was a completely furnished miniature house. Each piece of furniture was an exact small reproduction of an antique. There were tables, chairs, desks, and a washstand circa 1880. The washstand had doors that opened, as did the drawers in the desks and tables.

Ted is a slight, soft-spoken man, very modest about his magnificent craftsmanship. He took us down to his basement workshop and we watched him in action. He was using small knives to carve, and tweezers to handle bits and pieces. With the micrometer, he can turn spindles down to 65/1000ths of an inch. While he worked, his hand was as steady as a rock.

Lately, he's become interested in reproducing early Canadian furniture.

"I feel there's a long-term value," he said. "Just in case the originals are lost, future generations will have these small pieces of history."

Ted gets specifications from books on antique miniature furniture, but I found the replicas of the Robert's own antiques most interesting.

There's a bow-backed 1850 Windsor chair that Ted bought in Jackson's Point for $5 about 20 years ago. It's now valued at $1,200. And there's a slant-top desk once owned by Canada Steamship Lines.

He doesn't confine his craft to himself. Twice a week he goes to a Picton public school to teach children the fundamentals of making mini-furniture. And he designated a travelling case to carry some of his work to fairs and craft shows where he's a frequent guest.

Ted Roberts lives in two worlds. There's the one most of us live in — where we work or play, and often resent the hustle and bustle of modern life. But when Ted wants to get away from all that sort of thing, he just goes into his own small world.

The Gingerbread Man

🍎

There's a narrow brick building on Main Street in the village of Erin that has a certain elegance to it.

That's understandable. It's the home of Gotham Inc., makers of "gingerbread" — lacy whimsical decorative trim you often see on the gables and verandas of houses.

The houses are usually of the century-old variety that were built by settlers from England and the United States who brought the old folk art to Ontario in the mid-1800s. But before long you may see gingerbread on newer houses too.

That's partly because of Joe Colucci, an enterprising young man who is thought to be the only professional maker of authentic wooden gingerbread in the country.

People often refer to him now as "The Gingerbread Man". But he didn't imagine he would ever have such a nickname when he opened Gotham Inc. eight years ago.

He had been a sales executive in Toronto who gradually developed an interest in restoring houses. He and his wife Trish decided they could run a restoration business in the country just as easily as in the city, so they moved to Erin, south of Orangeville.

Colucci also developed an increasing interest in the gingerbread on the houses he was restoring. He thought he'd try and learn something more about it and include it in the business as a sideline. He and Trish figured it might make up about 5% of the business.

"I knew absolutely nothing about gingerbread, or about woodworking," says Colucci. "In fact, eight years ago, I didn't even own a hammer."

He got books on the subject, talked to a few woodworkers, got some tools, and through trial and error, began to turn out some fairly good pieces of gingerbread. He also discovered that although there was a big demand for it, no one else was making the authentic stuff. Before long, word got out and he was getting orders from people who wanted gingerbread restored, or in some cases, wanted him to dream up new designs for verandas, porches and gables of houses both old and new.

Colucci's original direction seemed to be taking a strange twist. So he trained four artisans in the craft. When we dropped around we saw him busily engaged in the company's basement workshop. I asked Joe why gingerbread had become so popular again. "It's all part of a larger movement," he told me. "People are returning to the past, especially in Victorian furniture and Gothic architecture. Possibly because of a desire for a more artistic lifestyle."

These days, despite the fact that Colucci and his cohorts have a hard time keeping up with the orders, they're not fretting about it. They're just floating along on the current wave of nostalgia.

Small Ships

❦

When the Collingwood Shipyards closed a few years ago, it was the end of an era. Everybody was sorry to see it go. Vern MacDuffie was one of them. He'd worked at the shipyard for 35 years.

But Vern did something about it. One night, when he was watching a story about "The Titanic" on television, he decided he's try to build a model of the ill-fated ocean liner.

He started from scratch. No plans, no kits, just a photograph. Of course, being an experienced electrician and woodworker helped. He's a wizard with wood and the Titanic model he made was something of a miniature masterpiece.

He went on to build the "City of Collingwood", one of the early steel boats built in the shipyards. A man from Georgian Peaks saw it and bought it for $700. Suddenly, Vern saw his hobby in a different light.

When I saw him, he had built 36 ships and was swamped with orders for more of them. Some he kept for himself. There's the "Sea Witch", just like the one Vern saw in an old Errol Flynn movie. Over in a corner of the living room is the "Chi-Cheemaun", the famed Tobermory ferry loaded with tiny cars and trucks.

"It was the hardest one to make," said Vern. "I had to take three runs at the bow because it curves in an unusual way."

His wife Gwen is as absorbed in the work as Vern. She paints the boats, does the tricky bits with sails and rigging, and comes up with a lot of imaginative ideas. It takes them about three weeks to complete one of the model ships.

I watched Vern cutting the one-inch lumber he uses. He was in the process of building a self unloader, a job that had been commissioned by the captain of the vessel.

The projects are taking up more and more of the MacDuffie's time. Gwen had to give up babysitting the grandchildren, and the couple are beginning to see a really big future in their small ships.

The Fall Guy

❦

Most of the time I live in the present or the near future. I'm not much for looking back on "the good old days".

But when the leaves change colour and begin drifting slowly toward the ground, a nostalgic spell starts to creep over me. It happens every year.

I think of coming in from playing football with a few friends (or "rugby" as we called it) in a small park near our house, to be greeted by the aroma of the chili sauce my mother was making. Or wandering in solitary splendour, kicking leaves. I can still hear the rustling beneath my boots.

One year, the leaves turned earlier than usual up around Muskoka, Haliburton, the Kawarthas and the area surrounding our farm where we see Southern Georgian Bay and Beausoleil Island from our kitchen window.

On a weekend when we were home, Jenny and I walked to our woodlot behind the farmhouse and kicked leaves in what our youngest grandchildren, Max and Eric, call The Green Forest. It was no longer green, of course, as we sauntered along collecting a few special leaves that appealed to us. The walk joined the other things in other autumns I'll always remember.

The next day Terry joined us and we went up to do a story about what's billed in Muskoka as the annual Cavalcade of Colour.

We started at High Falls near Bracebridge. Our friends David and Mary Brooks live nearby and Terry took shots of Mary, Jenny and Clementine, the Brooks' beautiful big Labrador Retriever, walking down a land with a background of red, yellow and russet leaves shimmering in the sunlight against the rugged pines.

Muskoka was in its Fall glory as we moved off to other areas. It was a great show. Produced by Mother Nature, Associate Producer Jack Frost and directed by Joe Chlorophyll, it was one of the best performances I've seen in years.

Later in the month we went to the Elmvale Fall Fair and saw the fruits of the harvest along with the other country things that have always made up the backbone of Ontario life.

A few days after that we were in the Lucan area doing a story about an ancient water-powered flour mill, then across to Norfolk country to check on the peanut harvest.

We got back to the farm for Thanksgiving and a big family dinner. The leaves in The Green Forest were at their peak.

I have nicknames for most of our children and grandchildren. Our daughter Andrea is The Good Fairy, son Roy is Hercules, granddaughter Robin is Miss Muffet, and her brother Bob is The Engineer. The list goes on and on.

My nostalgic spell swelled to gigantic proportions as I watched Jenny making applesauce just the way her mother made it. Miss Muffet and The Engineer were helping her.

Hercules was piling wood, the Good Fairy was raking the front lawn as our big maple tree released its coloured leaves that seemed to wave a fond farewell for another year.

I was thinking that as soon as my annual visit to the Royal Winter Fair is over the spell would be broken and I'd be back to normal. That is until next autumn when once again, I'll become The Fall Guy.

Huron Village

❦

The Indian Village, overlooking Little Lake in the Southern Georgian Bay town of Midland, is a reconstruction of how our native people lived 400 years ago.

Although every year hundreds of thousands of people visit Ste. Marie Among the Hurons and the Martyr's Shrine just a few miles away, the Indian Village is slightly off the beaten track and is rarely overcrowded. But it gives you a wealth of information about Huron life before the Europeans arrived.

The village was built in 1954 by an archaeological team from the University of Western Ontario, supervised by Wilf Jury, the expert who reconstructed Ste. Marie and many other historic sites.

It's completely authentic. The village is surrounded by palisades for defence, and near the entrance are examples of pottery and a graphic explanation of totem masks. Inside, when in season, there's a small patch of corn and another of tobacco. About 65% of their diet was made up of corn, augmented by berries and nuts. Tobacco had a spiritual significance and was believed to clear the head for deliberation at council.

Nearby is the Medicine Man's lodge with its masks and herbs. The Medicine Man was a spiritual advisor and administered herbs and ointments for ailments. Herbs were highly regarded for both prevention and cure of disease, as they are today by many people.

In another hut is the sweat bath, also thought to contribute to health. Beside the door was a fire where stones were heated, then rolled into the hut. After the bath, the Hurons ran to plunge into the nearest stream or roll in the snow.

The focal point of any village was the longhouse. It was a meeting place and also provided sleeping accommodation. In this village, bunks are covered with furs, and firewood stored below the bunks. In the centre of the building is a row of smouldering fires. Two families shared each fire. Children learned from example — the girls to pound corn and other household duties, the boys to shoot bows and arrows and to fish.

Near the longhouse is an Algonquian type birchbark canoe. Bark was secured to white cedar ribs by hemlock gum and pitch. A Huron could travel over 50 miles a day by canoe.

Along the way, I learned an interesting titbit of information from one of the guides. The name "Huron" isn't an Indian name at all. The people called themselves "Quendat". The early French explorers coined the term "Huron".

Elderhostel

❦

We visited an Elderhostel one day. It happened to be at Geneva Park near Orillia. But it could have been in Maine or Manitoba or Wales or Greece. There are 1,200 locations in 45 countries available as Elderhostels. They're a fairly recent development in travel, adventure and education for seniors or "elders".

The idea was sparked by the success and popularity of Youth Hostels in Europe where travelling students can get inexpensive accommodation. Elderhostels added an additional twist. They offered brief courses of study in five or six day stays at a college campus, conference centre or something similar. Like the Youth Hostels, accommodation was inexpensive.

The first one was started in 1975 in the United States. The thing spread like wildfire. Now there are long waiting lists of seniors wanting to attend Elderhostels. Part of the popularity is a desire to travel and meet people. But it's much deeper than that. It's a desire to learn. Just for the fun of it.

The elders study everything from Cicero to computers and from politics to poetry. They exchange ideas. They attend seminars and lectures given by experts who volunteer their services.

There were about 40 attending the Elderhostel at Geneva Park, a big camp and conference centre on Lake Couchiching. They came from all walks of life. Some were Ph.D's, some were high school dropouts. But they had two things in common. They were all 60 or over, and all had a love of learning.

We dropped in on a seminar called "The Origins of Lake Couchiching". There were charts and maps all over the place. It was being conducted by a brilliant, witty little old man with a beard who reminded me of one of the seven Dwarfs. Later, there was to be a walk around parts of the lake.

We went outside and caught up with a group studying what was billed as "Exploring the World at Your Feet". It was a nature course designed to tune up your powers of observation.

The third course was about Canadian Humour, and a trip to the nearby Stephen Leacock Home was on the agenda.

We spent the morning at the Elderhostel. The whole atmosphere was of vibrant interest — in life and in learning.

This year alone, 200,000 elders have enrolled in courses in various parts of the world. Which puts the damper on that ancient fallacy that you can't teach an old dog new tricks.

The Impossible Dream

❦

When Marilyn Oldfield decided to start a holiday resort for the disabled, people told her that she was "just plain nuts". They should have known better. Marilyn knew what she was doing. Her experiences as a nurse, and her entrepreneurial instincts told her the idea was a natural.

True, she didn't have much money, and couldn't get a government grant because there was no precedent for such a scheme. But she had a good credit rating and managed to scrape up $150,000 to buy some land and a ramshackle house near Pefferlaw, on Lake Simcoe.

She also had a lot of friends who volunteered to help her rebuild the old house and cut out a few nature trails through the heavily-forested areas on the property.

Everything was geared to wheelchair accessibility. Light switches and counters in the house were lower, electrical outlets higher, doorways wider and there were many floor-to-ceiling windows.

That was eight years ago. These days you see people in wheelchairs coming and going among the three miles of paved nature trails, stopping to gaze at wildflowers or watch chipmunks scurry across a path. You see people plying horseshoes, fishing in a pond stocked with rainbow trout, swaying back and forth in a specially-designed garden swing, or going up convenient ramps into one of the housekeeping cottages that have been built up near the renovated old house.

It's a year-round resort and not necessarily confined to the disabled. Families and friends of the regular guests often visit, and there are vacationers who stay there just because it's a nice quiet resort.

"I don't expect to make a fortune," smiles Marilyn, whose easy-going style belies her tremendous vitality. "We've geared prices so that a handicapped person on a disability pension can afford it. I'm only looking to make expenses. The disabled have the same needs as others. If other people can go camping, why can't they? It improves their quality of life."

Marilyn calls the resort "Eaglewood" because, as she puts it, "the eagle is a bird that knows no barriers."

And, although it may have seemed like an impossible dream at first, the dream came true. Not only for Marilyn Oldfield, but for hundreds of handicapped people who now have a place such as they never had before, where they can have a holiday in the country.

Stenning's Steeds

❦

Bill Stenning started working with Conklin's Carnival when he was 17 years old. He helped operate the merry-go-round. Today, he's a London businessman and entrepreneur, but he never lost interest in carousels and has a valuable collection of antique carousel animals.

I dropped in to say hello to him at his automobile business on Trafalgar Street, and found him restoring merry-go-round animals for Guelph's Riverside Park Carousel.

It was a big job. A shop in the garage was chock-full of horses and one pig. Stenning had been working for months getting the animals ready for the spring opening at Guelph.

I guess you could say that Bill, although now in his mid-sixties, never really left the carnival. When you get talking to him, he lapses into "carny" language. He mentions "forty-milers" and "donikers" and "brownies". The latter are hundred dollar bills.

"This horse," said Bill, stroking one of the refurbished horses, "is an original 1895 Armitage Hershell. It would cost plenty of brownies today."

The current value of the carousel animals is surprising. When merry-go-rounds are broken up, there's always an auction, invariably attended by hundreds of collectors. It's not unusual for an antique horse to fetch $150,000.

"Some of these Guelph pieces were real basket cases," said Bill. "We had to strip them of paint, fix the joints, and dig the rot out of the old timers. But now they're back in shape."

Most of the animals had been crated and were ready to be shipped back to their Riverside home.

"Here's one," said Bill pointing to a magnificent horse with flaring nostrils. "It was built as a four-on-the-floor, but was later converted to an up-and-downer."

I nodded wisely. But I was thinking how much joy the small animals bring. And how they represent so many magical childhood moments as you whirl through a myriad of lights while perched atop a fiery steed.

Buggy Days

❧

I thought that when I grew old I'd become wise. But I'm not. I thought I'd become nostalgic and like to talk a lot about "the good old days". But I don't.

Then I went up to see a collection of buggies, wagons and carriages in Markham and was carried back to childhood.

A red T. Eaton Co. delivery wagon of the kind that used to rumble around Toronto streets drawn by well-groomed horses, swept me back to the early twenties.

The rest of the collection was a few years before my time, so my nostalgia spree was short-lived. However, it was enough to set me off on a stroll into another century.

My guide was John Mitchell, an exhibit designer who created realistic settings for the wonderful old conveyances, even to the types of roads they thundered and clattered over in bygone days.

They're housed at the Markham Museum in a big building with a brick facade emulating a carriageworks of the turn-of-the-century Markham Village. And the forty-eight relics of the road, known as the "Ward Collection", are a transportation historian's dream.

The centre piece is a horsecart used by Toronto butcher William Ward in the 1890s. His three sons resurrected and repaired it in 1944 and then began a search for other old carts, carriages, wagons and buggies.

They scoured the Ontario countryside and brought them back to their Markham Township farm for restoration. Last year, they donated them to the Museum.

Designer Mitchell has done impressive things with the collection. There's a heavy farm wagon being pulled by a life-like horse over a road made of logs — the so-called "corduroy" roads. There are buggies and "democrats" (the forerunners of station wagons) on what were known as "plank" roads. There's a big black coach that carried the mail from Pembroke to Ottawa in the 1860s. It's set on a gravel road, which was considered quite advanced.

Apparently, winter was thought to be the best time to travel, and after taking a look at a few of the roads, you can understand why. A cushion of snow or even slush would be better than some of those bone crushers.

As we roamed around the display the designer was telling me that one of the settlers' biggest complaints was about roads.

Toll roads were a nuisance. The corduroy roads would shake the bejabbers out of you. On top of that was the infernal mud!

Later, as I was driving away from the Museum, I mused about the wondrous changes that had been wrought by technology since the early settlers first arrived.

I thought about our sleek, speedy automobiles and our complex multi-laned highways. Then, as I was turning into a restaurant parking lot, I hit a pothole!

I muttered to myself. Then managed a slight chuckle. I guess some things never change.

Wildflower Garden

❧

Wildflowers rarely dress in showy garb. They come as they are to nature's annual gathering of floral clans. Ordinarily, they're not organized either. They turn up willy-nilly as the spirit moves them. They're the casual free-wheeling types.

But a group of seniors in the Huronia district decided to round up and organize several different kinds of wildflowers and plant them in a big garden they created at the Wye Marsh Wildlife Centre near Midland.

The group, called Seniors For the Wye Marsh, began planning the garden a couple of years ago, and turned a grassy knoll near the entrance of the Centre into a magnificent display. The wildflowers, although free spirits by nature, don't seem to mind it a bit. After all, they never had it better. They were transplanted from obscurity, are pampered by seniors and admired by hundreds of visitors.

There are 120 seniors involved in the project and they care for the garden in small groups. When I was there, about 10 were at work, including a 96-year-old lady who was planting a fern. The president of the club, Verna Ives, of nearby Waubaushene, led me down the garden paths to view the 41 varieties of flowers and show me how they had been divided into sections.

One of them is made up of plants which attract birds and insects. There's wild flox and Jerusalem artichokes. Verna pointed to some Queen Anne's Lace. "You'll notice," she said, "that among the tiny white flowers, there's a single black one. A small fly going by will think it's another fly and land to investigate. It gets pollen on its toes and carries it to the next plant. It's one of nature's tricks."

Another section features flowers common to Simcoe County, like the Tansy, Black Eyed Susan and the May Weed which looks similar to a She Loves Me, She Loves Me Not Daisy.

In another area are herbs. There's the Bee Bomb, loved by hummingbirds especially. Most of the herbs are of a kind used by the early settlers.

The seniors are in tune with the times. Apparently, wildflower gardens are all the rage these days, especially in urban centres. And even gardening centres are beginning to carry wildflower seeds. So no matter where you live you can now have wildflowers in your backyard from early in March to late in October.

Retirement Home For Horses

❧

Have you ever interviewed a horse? Well, it requires a certain journalistic technique. I did it through an interpreter named Dennis Taylor who operates a retirement home for horses near the village of Campbellville.

The retirement home, called Twitmarsh Farm, is located in a beautiful country setting. There are 150 acres of rolling hills and green pastures where aging horses can spend their golden years away from the pressures of the track or show ring.

The oldest horse there was 29-year-old Robin, who in his younger years had been with the Metro Toronto Mounted Police. When I first saw him, he was casually cantering around one of the green pastures. Dennis called out to him and he veered over toward us. I had made an appointment, so he knew why I was there.

He was a big brown horse who exuded a quiet confidence. He nodded slightly and gave me a smile showing his large white teeth the way wolves and tigers and guard dogs do. Some people regard that as a threatening gesture. The truth is, they're all just smiling as a greeting. The only polite thing to do is smile back. Try it sometime. If you're still around, give me a call and tell me how it worked out.

Anyway, after a few introductory remarks, Robin launched into a brief story of his life. "I've seen it all," he said. "The riots, the crowd control at parades and rock concerts, in and out among strike breakers, the traffic noise of Yonge Street. And when I was a rookie, I went through that tough training. I can tell you a police horse's lot is not a happy one, as the saying goes."

"But there were the good times, too," he went on to say. "The times when my partners would ride me down into Rosedale Ravine on a spring morning when the leaves were just beginning to burst forth."

He smiled again. "However, these are the best days of all," he said. "Here at Twitmarsh I just loaf around. I have big quarters with a southern exposure, regular inoculations and all that. And I have quite a few buddies here in my own age group. You just can't beat it."

Dennis was telling me that he and his wife Anne started the retirement home when they couldn't find a suitable place for their own aging horses. He showed me around.

In another building there were some younger horses. Most of them were race horses, there for a brief holiday to get away from it all. In a way, the farm is a sort of spa for horses.

Before I left, I went back to say goodbye to Robin. He gave me a horselaugh as we parted. If you're inclined to regard the interview with some scepticism, please be assured I got it straight from the horse's mouth.

Where's the Fish?

❦

I go ice fishing once a year. I've never caught anything. I only go to do an annual story. It's a tradition. And I shiver every time I think of this year's excursion, which took place at Waubaushene on the shores of Southern Georgian Bay.

Cold? You betcha! I've been in bush country in Northern Ontario in the dead of winter. I've been in Frobisher Bay, and even in Greenland during the coldest winter they'd had in 100 years. But never, never, have I felt such bone-rattling cold as that February day in Waubaushene. The temperature wasn't really that bad. It was -25 degrees celsius, but the wind chill factor made it about -48 degrees celsius. And it had a mean streak in it that made even the experienced outdoor types I was with shake in their mukluks.

We had met at the Wild Duck Restaurant on Highway 69, which leads up to Parry Sound. The idea was to do a TV item about the joys of ice fishing. There were six of us — Roy, Bruce, Paul, Ernie, cameraman Terry, and myself. Two of the boys had fish huts out on the ice about a mile away from the restaurant.

Ernie had been out earlier to check on things, and wasn't too happy about going back. "There's no way I'm going out there again," he said. "The snow has drifted and the Northwest cuts right through you. It's murder on that ice."

Terry and I have seldom walked away from a story because of weather, and Bruce, who had driven up from the city, didn't want to waste the day. We talked it over and finally convinced Ernie to go along.

We had four snowmobiles. I rode behind Ernie's machine in a small sled known as a "skiboose". Roy lent me his balaclava to cover my face, and headed for his snowmobile. About two minutes later, he came back. One side of his face was white from the whipping wind. "I'll have to take that back," he shouted over the roar of the engines. "Here's a blanket to hold over your face."

Our wild ride began again. As we hit the drifts, the skiboose flew up and then down in a series of thuds, shaking the bejabbers out of me.

When we arrived at the huts, Terry got his equipment set up to shoot pictures. One of the huts was fairly primitive, but the other was more elaborate and had vinyl siding — strictly Royal York as fishing huts go. We lit the small stove and got the tippers ready. We wanted to show how to cut a hole in the ice. We went outside in the bitter cold, but the gas auger wouldn't work, and Paul had to use an axe.

I was to interview Bruce on why he enjoyed ice fishing. We had to leave the door open so that Terry could get enough light, and the cruel Northwest came driving in around the corner of the hut. We began the interview.

"It's the solitude and the quiet," said Bruce, as the wind whistled around. You could see his breath, and his teeth were chattering.

Terry took a couple of shots of us pretending to fish. Then we packed everything up and got out of there fast.

Back at the restaurant, huddled over coffee, we began to see the humour of the whole thing. We started to relax. No rush, no fuss, no fish.

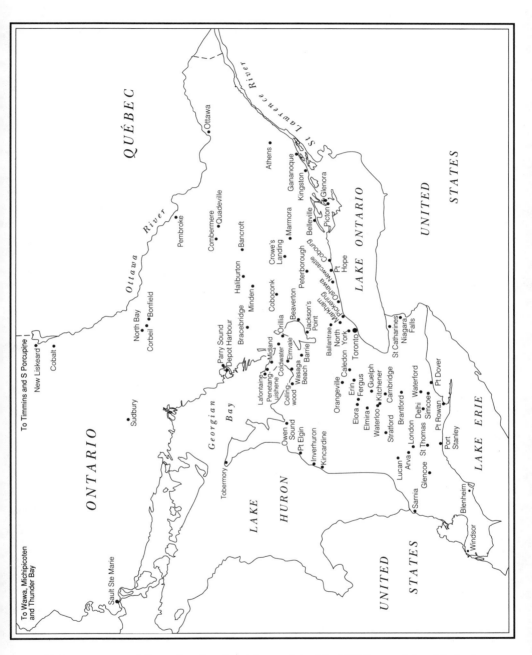

Reference map of Ontario, showing places visited by Bill Bramah in this book.